I0390425

Alphabetical Animals
A Coloring Book for Adults

By Olivia Goguen © 2016

This book is dedicated to the love of my life, Ethan, for always believing in me. And to Ethan's mom, Devrie, and brother, Preston, for helping me to get on my way and publish my first coloring book.

Images were obtained from public domain locations, and credited where necessary. Most of the initial information about the various animals was found from the website A-Z Animals (http://a-z-animals.com/animals/). Additional information is listed under each colorable image. Enjoy!

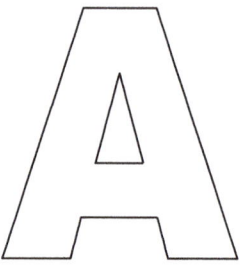

Antelope

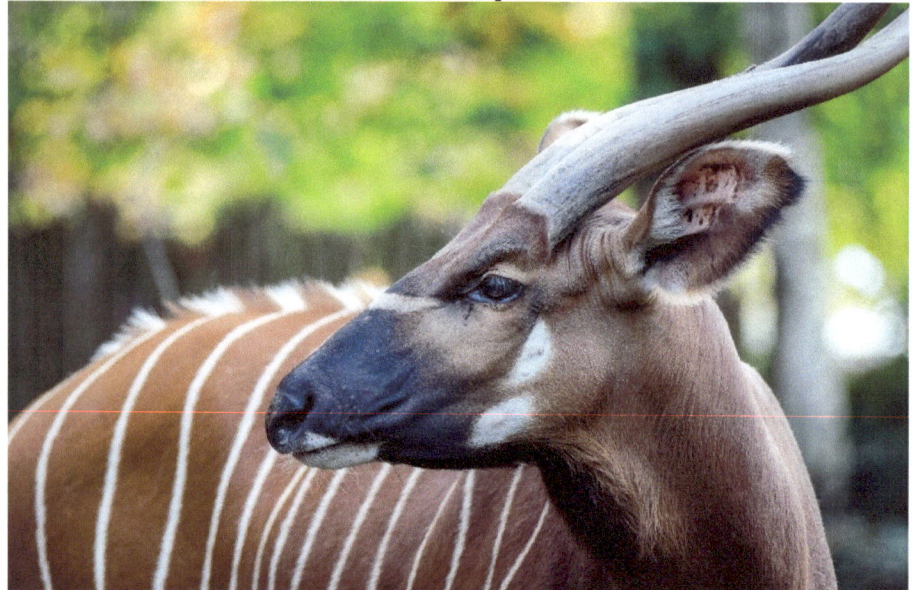

This image is of a Bongo Antelope which are only found in rainforests with dense undergrowth across the tropical parts of Africa.

Antelope come in a variety of different species including the tiny Royal Antelope that stands at the height of a rabbit!

(African Wildlife Foundation, Bongo, http://www.awf.org/wildlife-conservation/bongo)

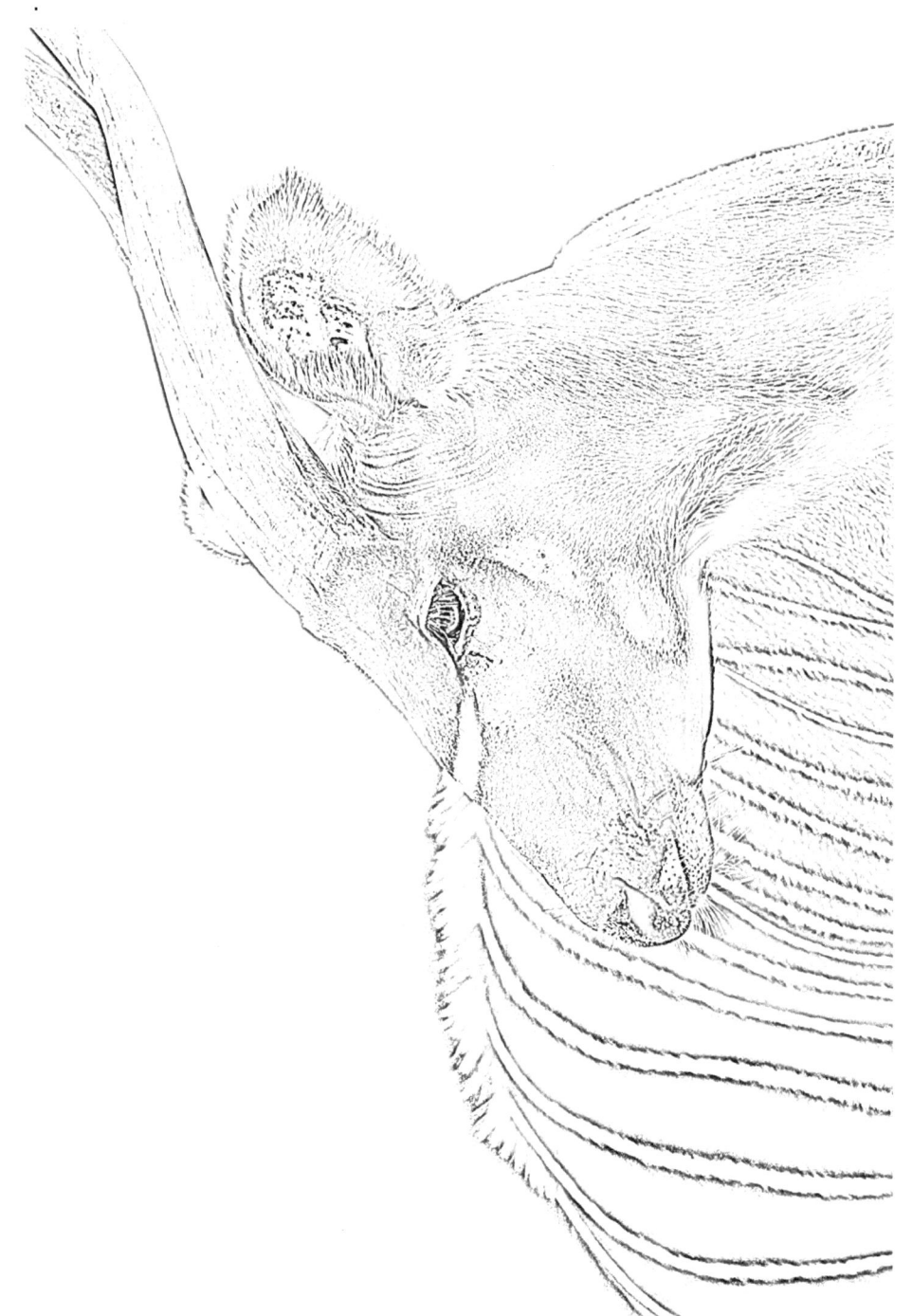

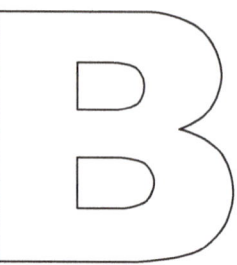

Booby

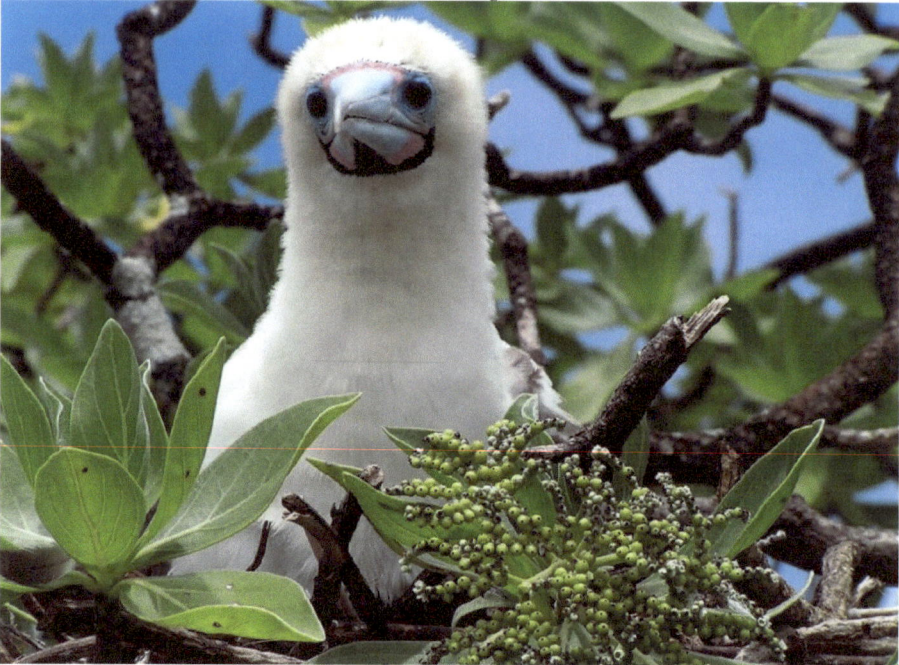

This image is of a red-footed booby chick, existing to the second largest colony of red-footed boobies in the world located on an uninhibited island 1,000 miles south of Hawaii known as Palmyra Atoll.

The most commonly found large sea-bird on the Galapagos Islands, the booby spends most of its life hunting fish at sea.

(US Fish and Wildlife Services, Palmyra Atoll, http://www.fws.gov/refuge/Palmyra_Atoll/wildlife_and_habitat/index.html)

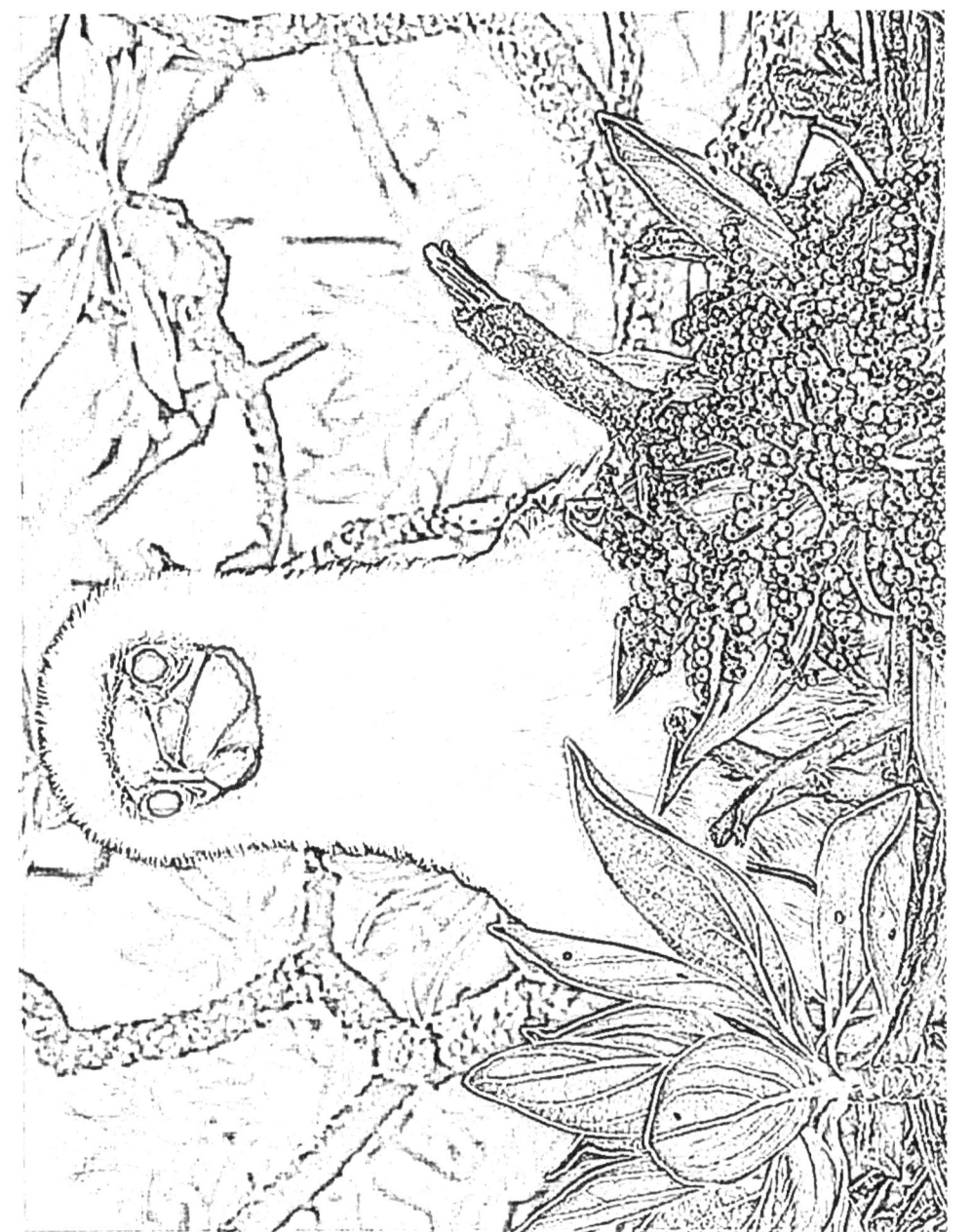

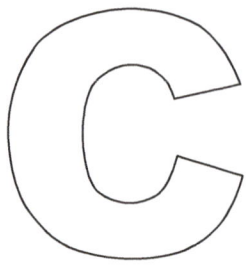

Cuttlefish

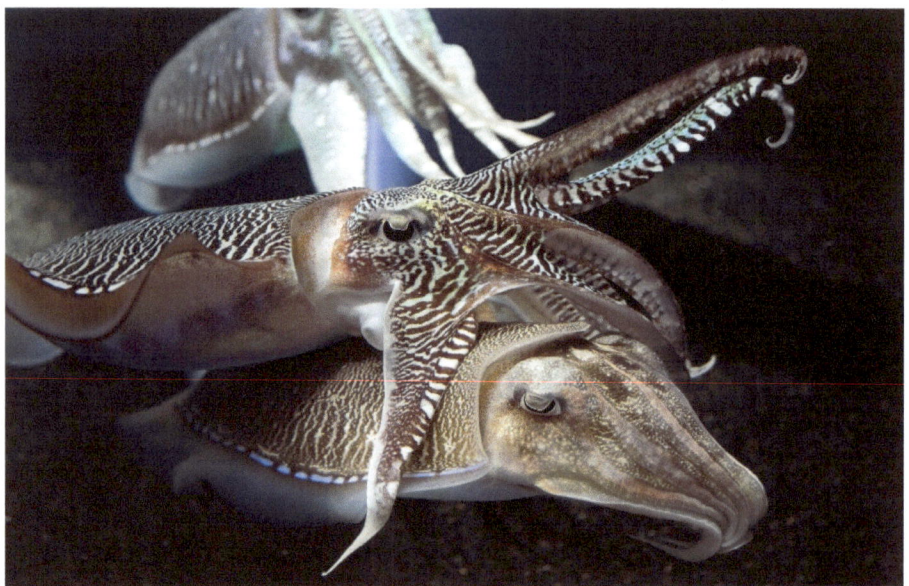

This image is of a cuttlefish which can be found at the Georgia Aquarium in Atlanta, Georgia.

Similar to a chameleon, the cuttlefish can change its color in an attempt to catch prey and is known for its "flashing" colors during the process of mating and fighting.

(http://www.georgiaaquarium.org/)

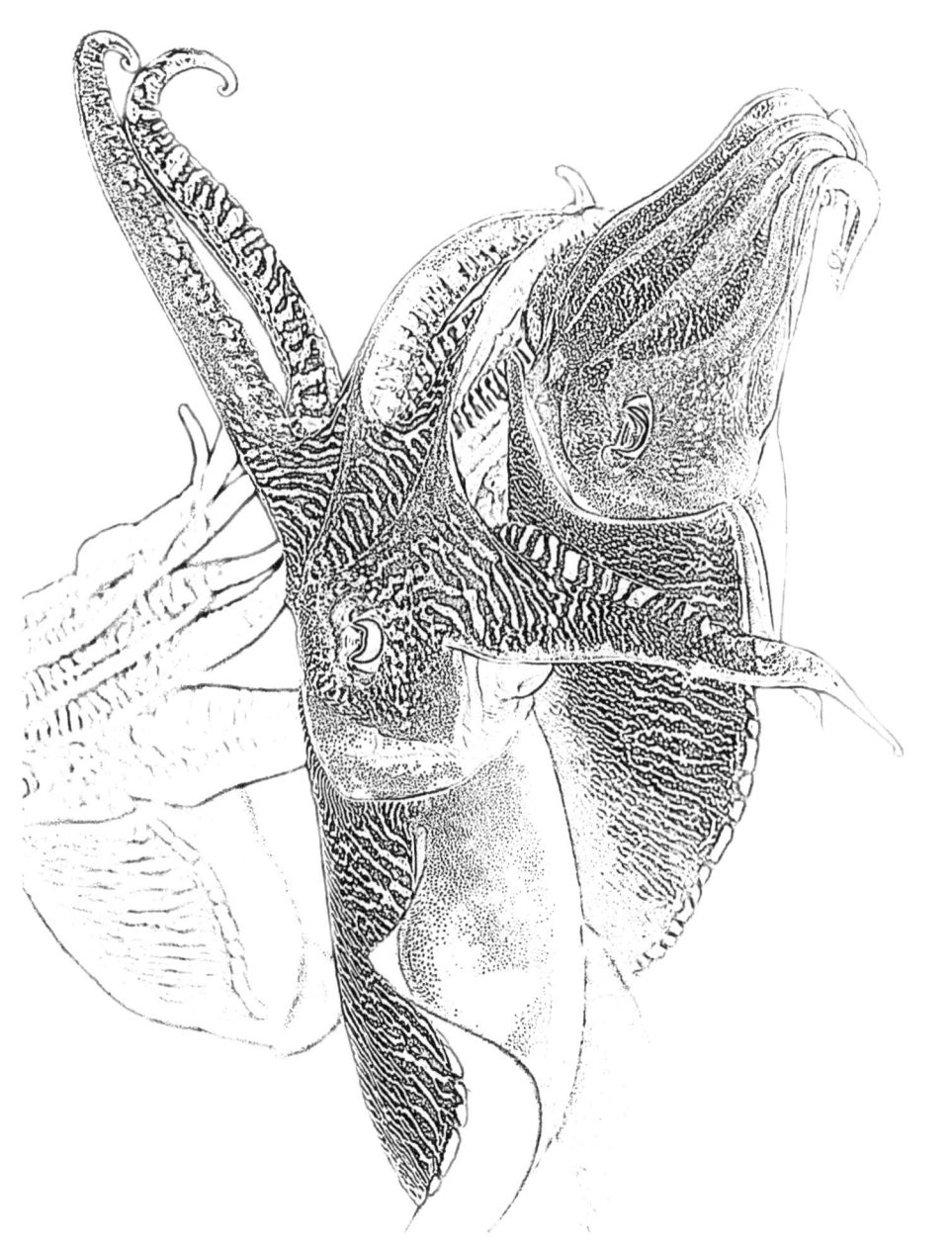

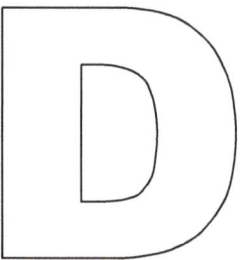

Dolphin

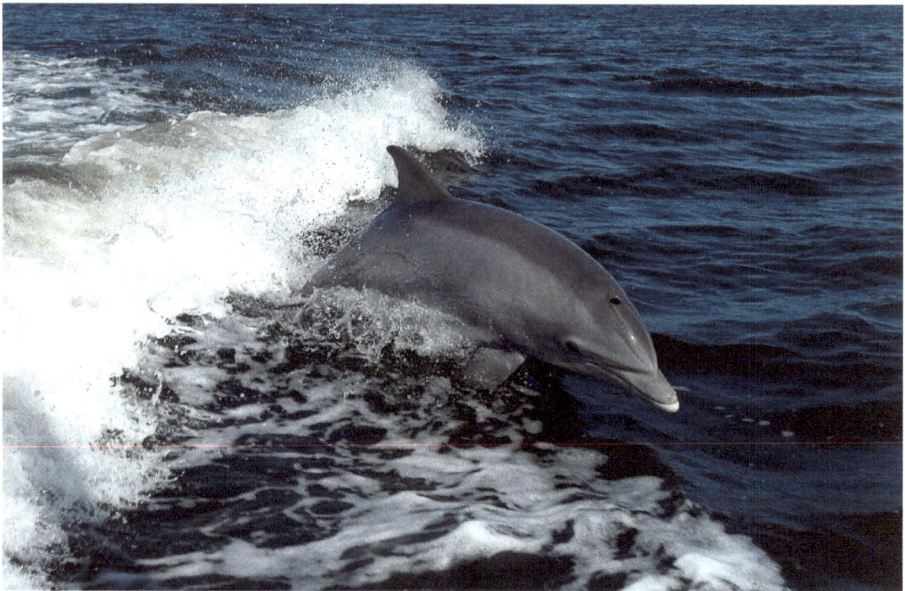

This image is of a Bottlenose Dolphin leaping out of the waves.

Dolphins are incredibly intelligent and social creatures, communicating with a complex system of whistles and squeaks. It is said they can make up to 1,000 clicking noises per second.

(National Geographic, Bottlenose Dolphin, http://animals.nationalgeographic.com/animals/mammals/bottlenose-dolphin/)

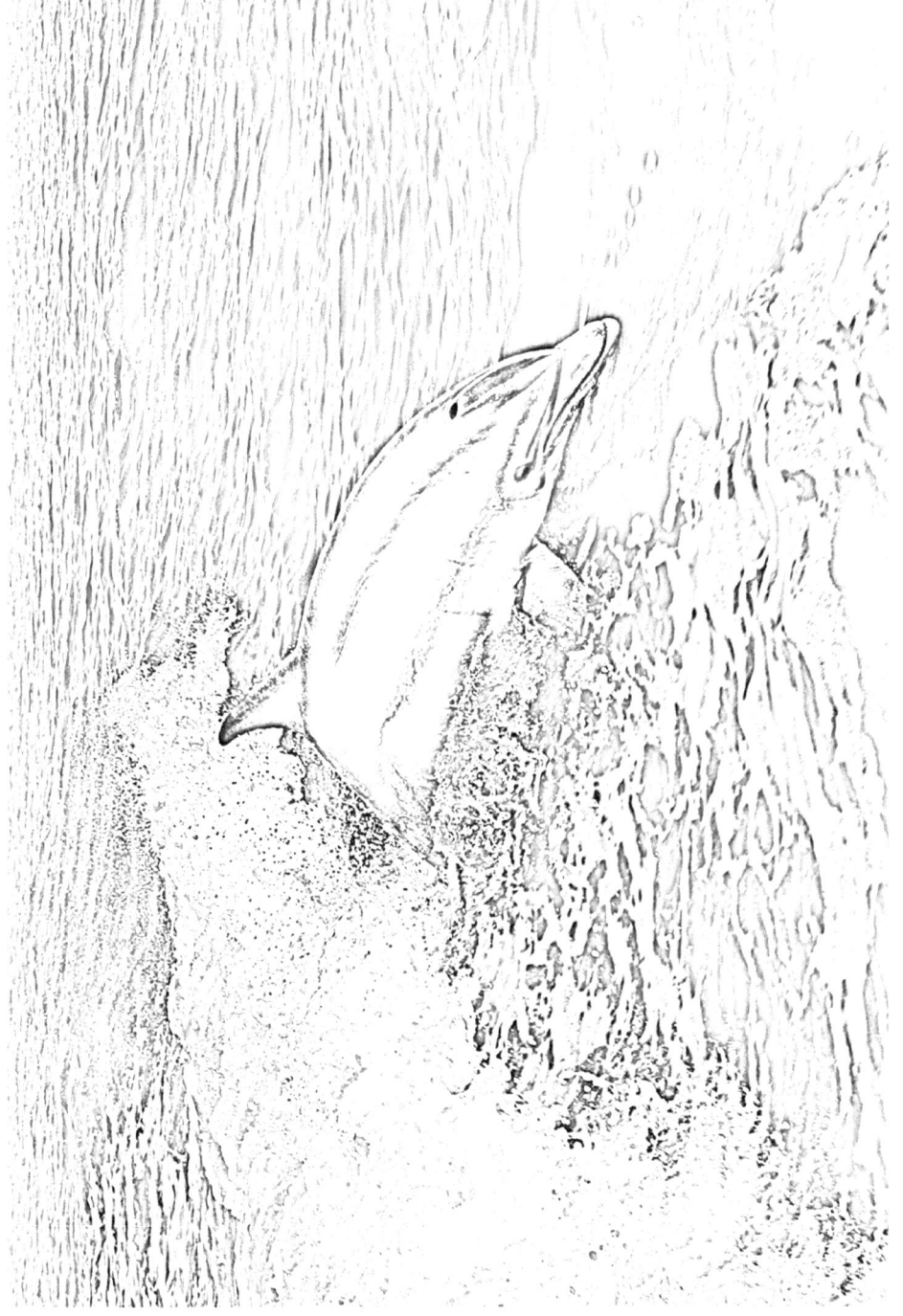

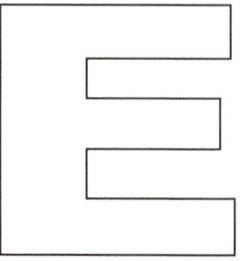

Eel

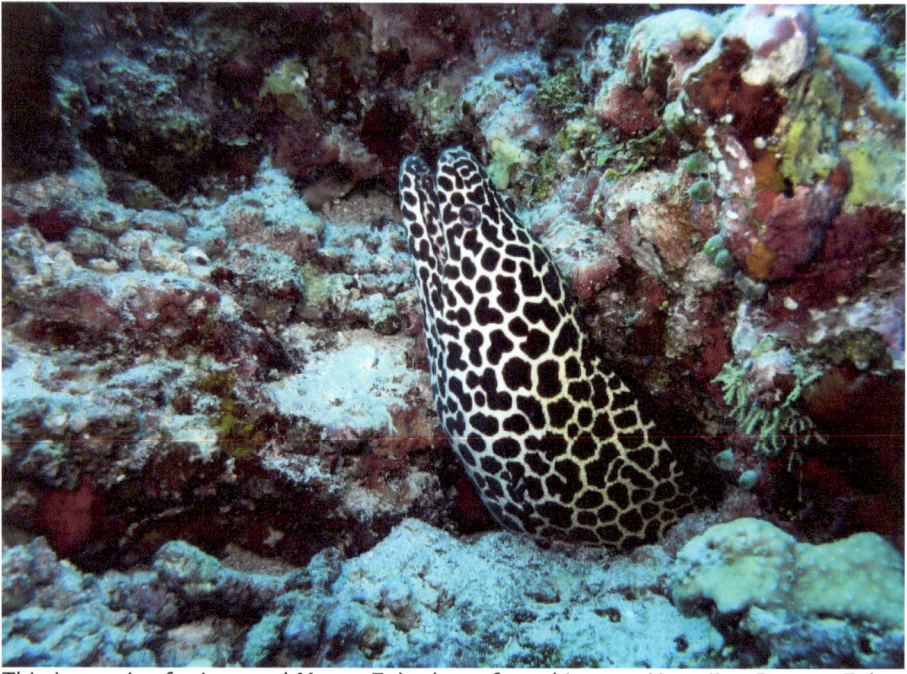

This image is of a Leopard Moray Eel, also referred to as a Hawaiian Dragon Eel or a Dragon Moray Eel, is a nocturnal creature preferring more temperate waters.

Eels are known to have very sharp teeth and there are species that can live in both fresh water and saltwater.

(Leopard Moray Eel, http://www.fish-species.org.uk/saltwater-fish/06-leopard-moray-eel.htm)

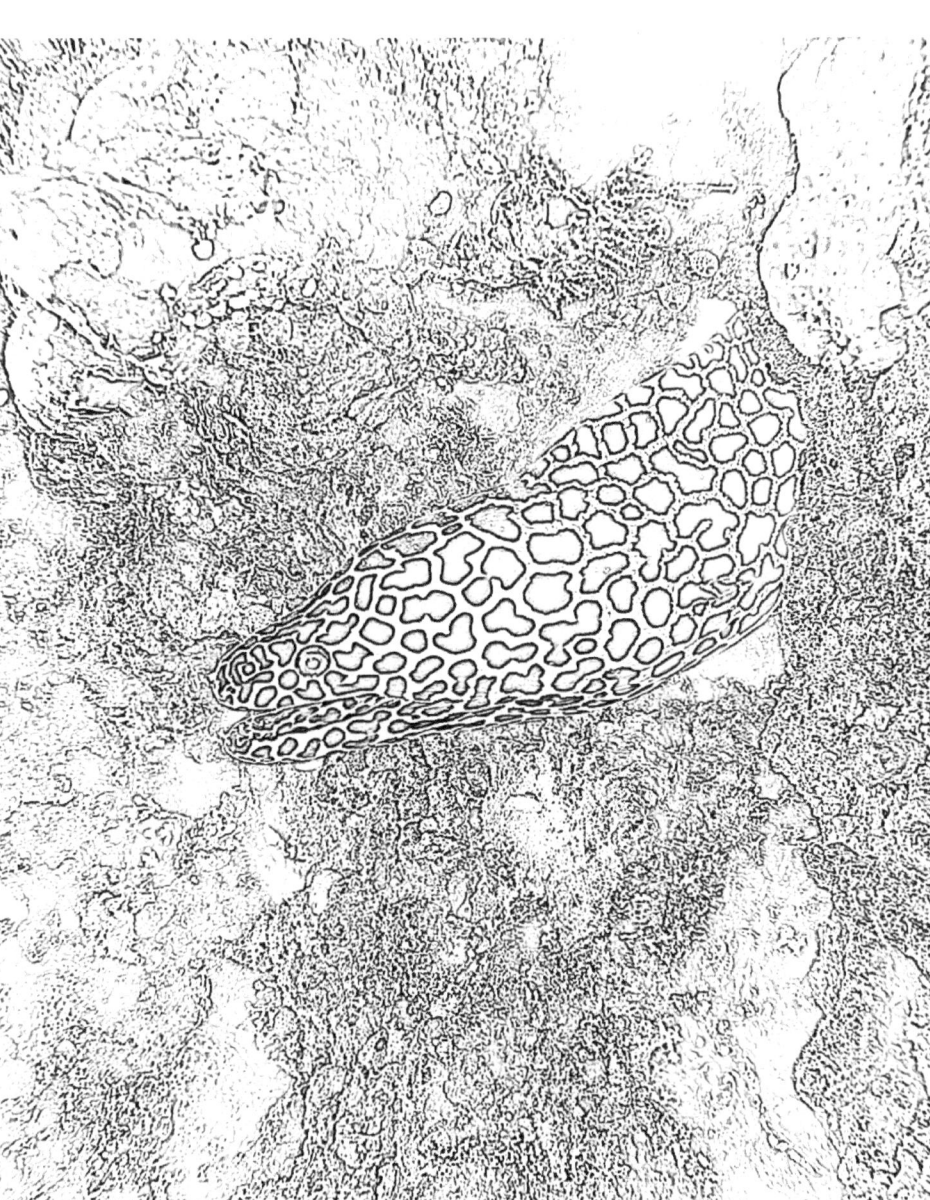

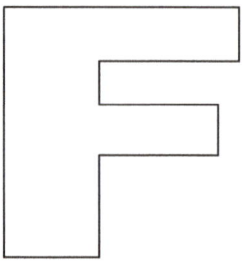

Frog

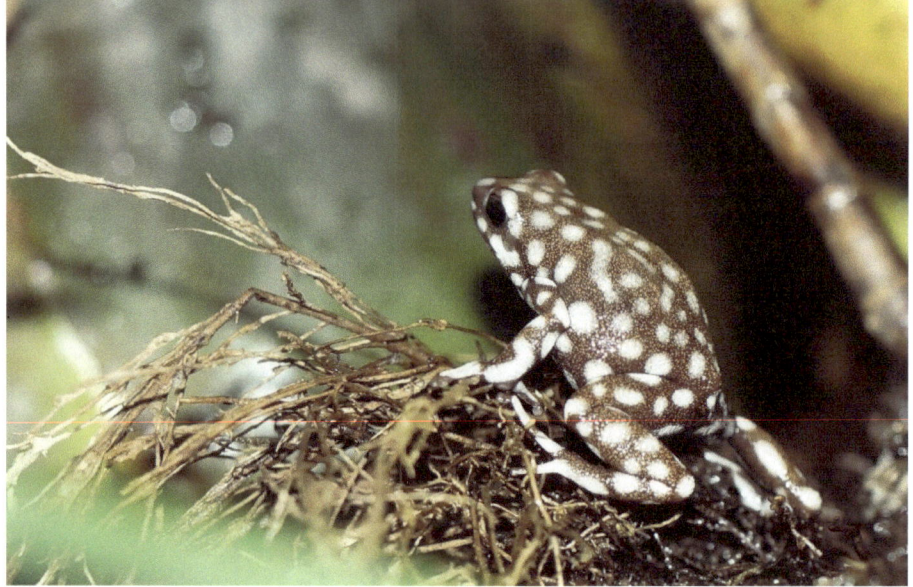

This image is of a Marañón Poison Frog, native only to the Santa Monica area of Peru and found to be endangered.

Frogs are amphibians which means they can live both on land and in water. Frogs can be found all around the world, excluding the Polar Regions.

(Amphibia Web, Excidobates mysteriosus, http://amphibiaweb.org/species/163)

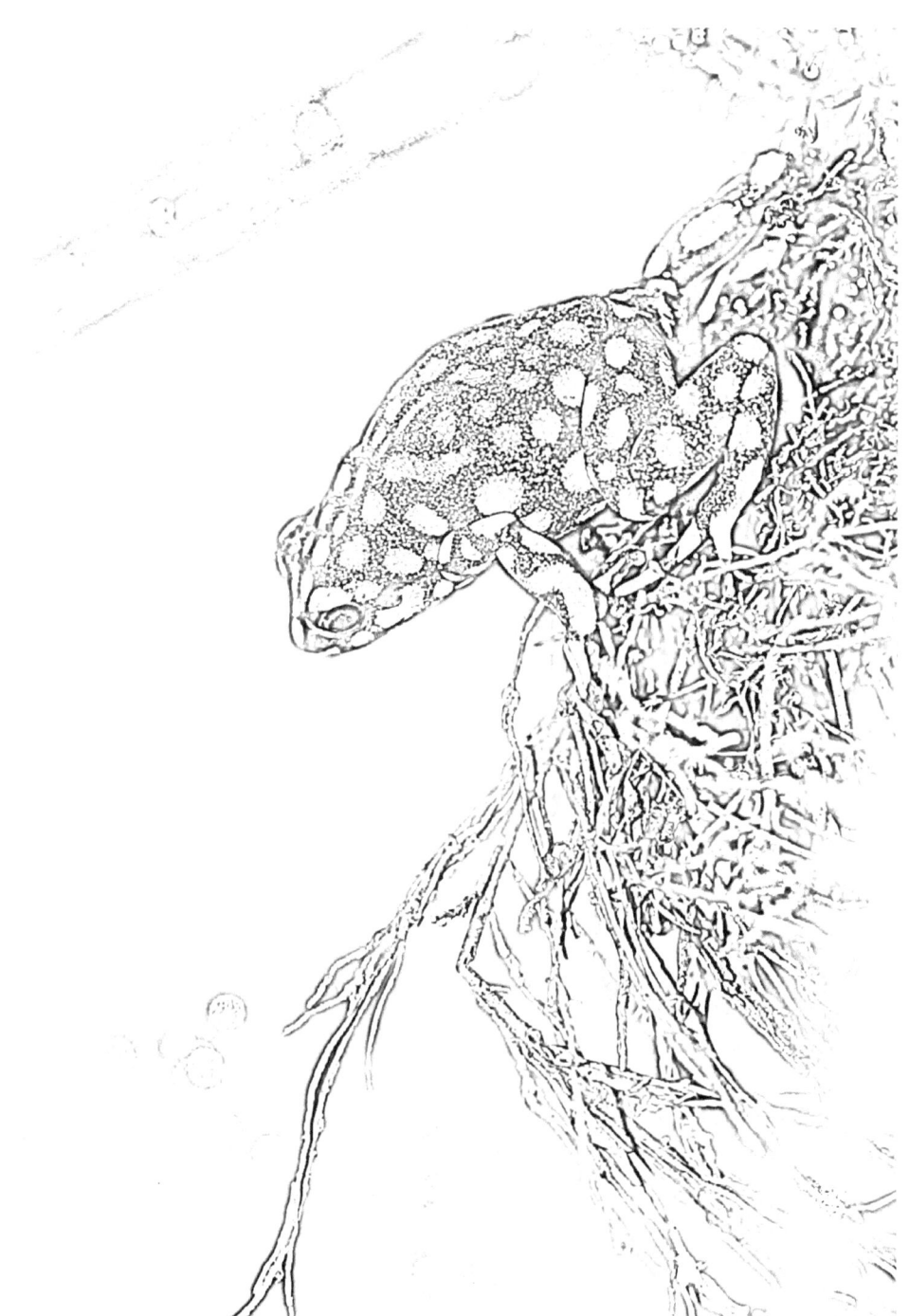

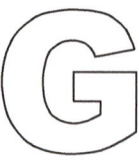

Giraffe

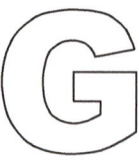

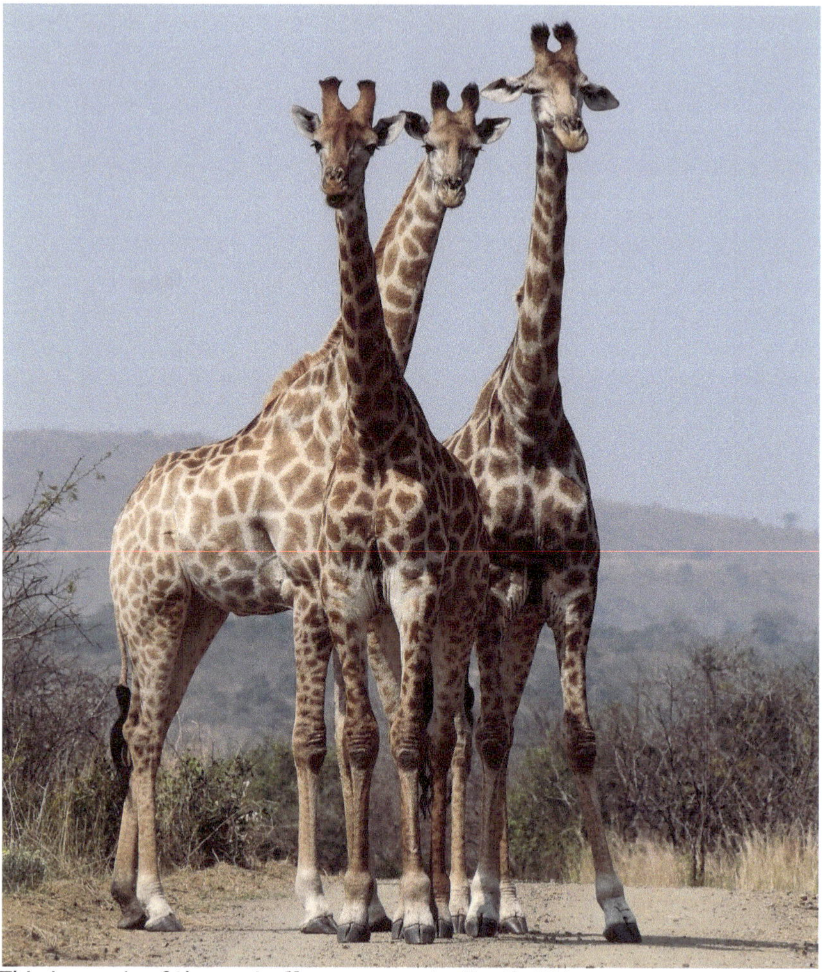

This image is of three giraffes common to South Africa.

Giraffes are the tallest living animal on land and also have the largest range of vision of all other land animals due in part to their height as well their large, sensitive eyes.

(National Geographic, Giraffe,
http://animals.nationalgeographic.com/animals/mammals/giraffe/)

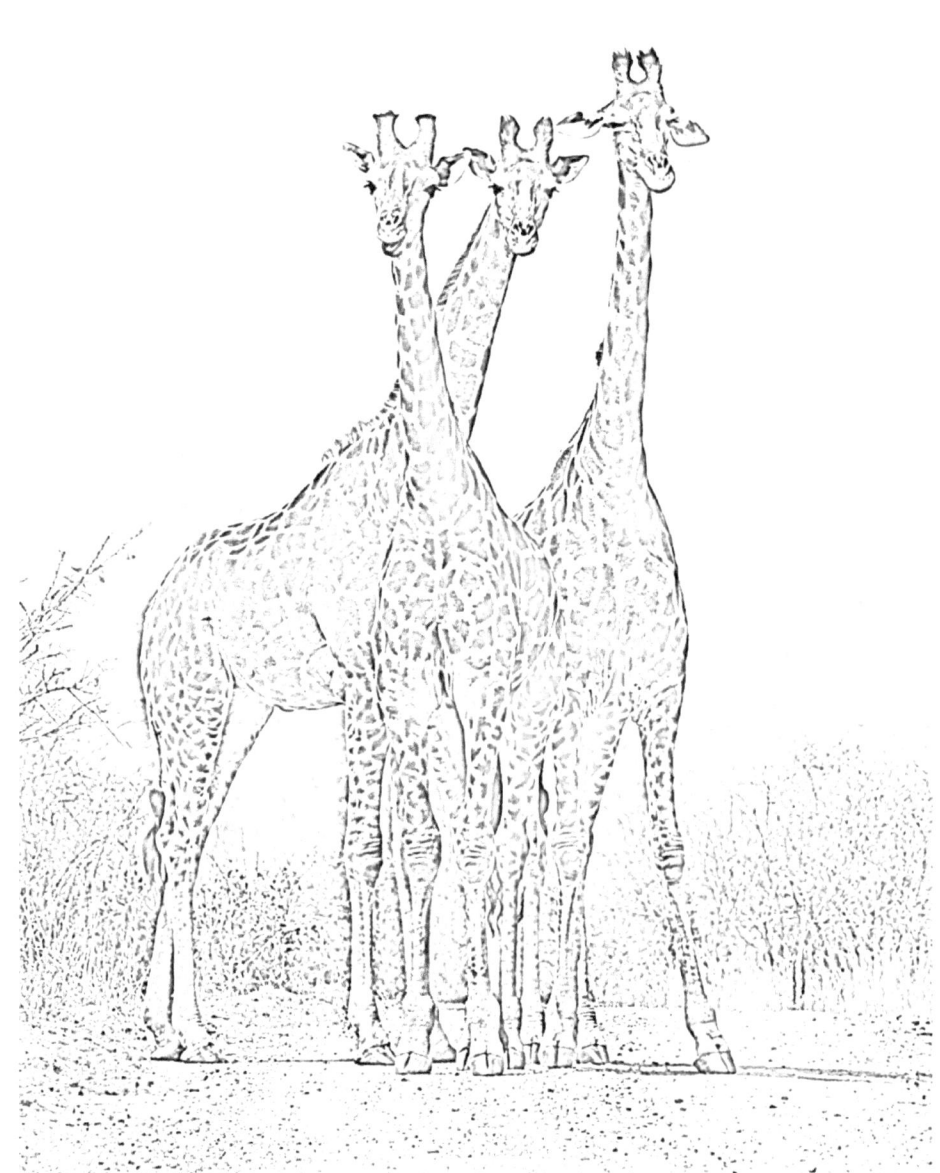

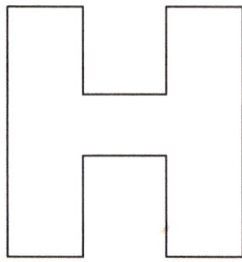

Humpback Whale

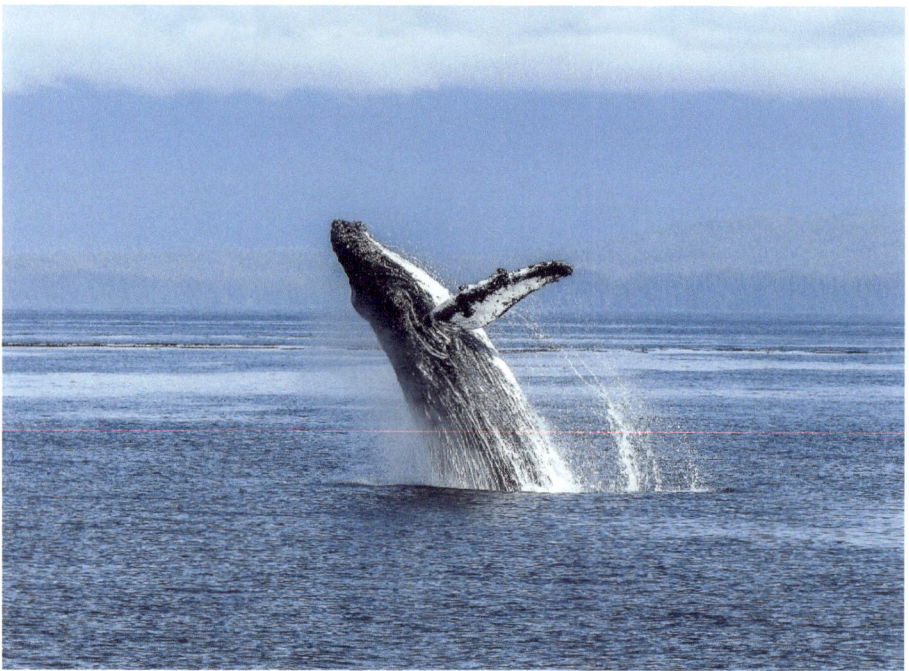

This image is of a Humpback Whale launching itself out of the water around Nova Scotia, Canada.

The Humpback Whale is a type of Baleen whale, meaning it does not have teeth, but instead has rows of plates. Its primary source of food is krill and plankton, though it's known to eat small fish and crabs that get filtered through as well.

(National Geographic, Humpback Whale, http://animals.nationalgeographic.com/animals/mammals/humpback-whale/)

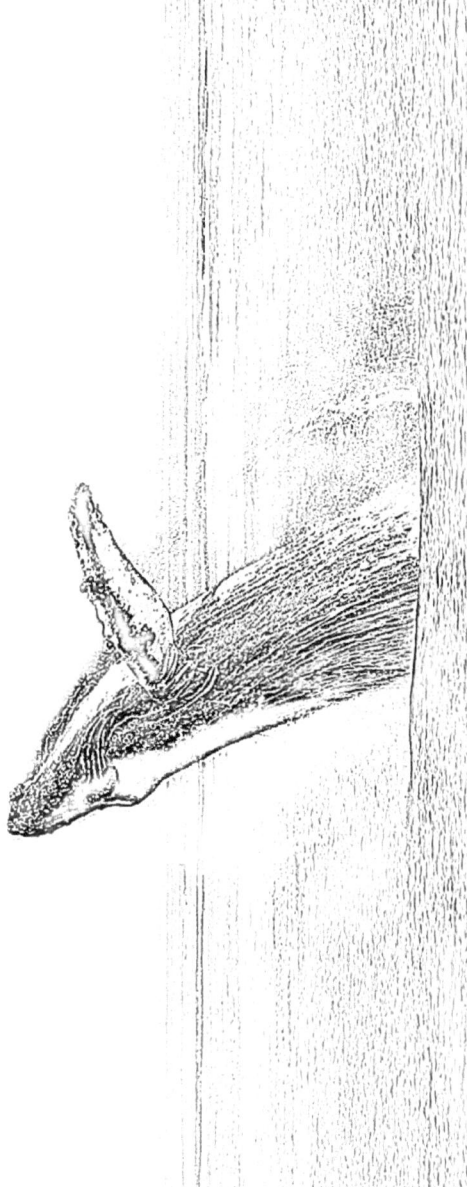

Iguana

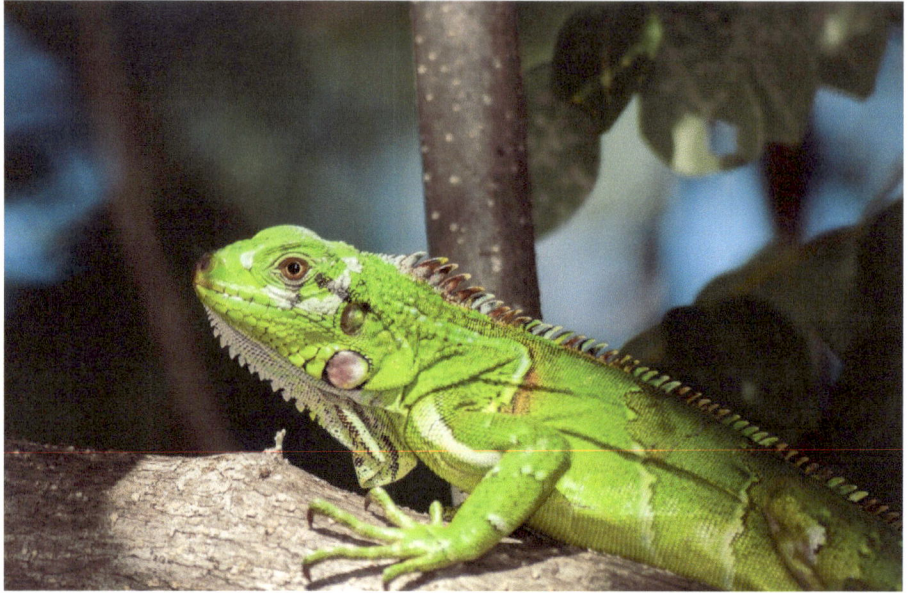

This image is of a Green Iguana which typically live in the treetops of the South American Rainforest.

Iguanas have amazing sight which not only allows them to detect predators, but allows them to communicate through various visual cues.

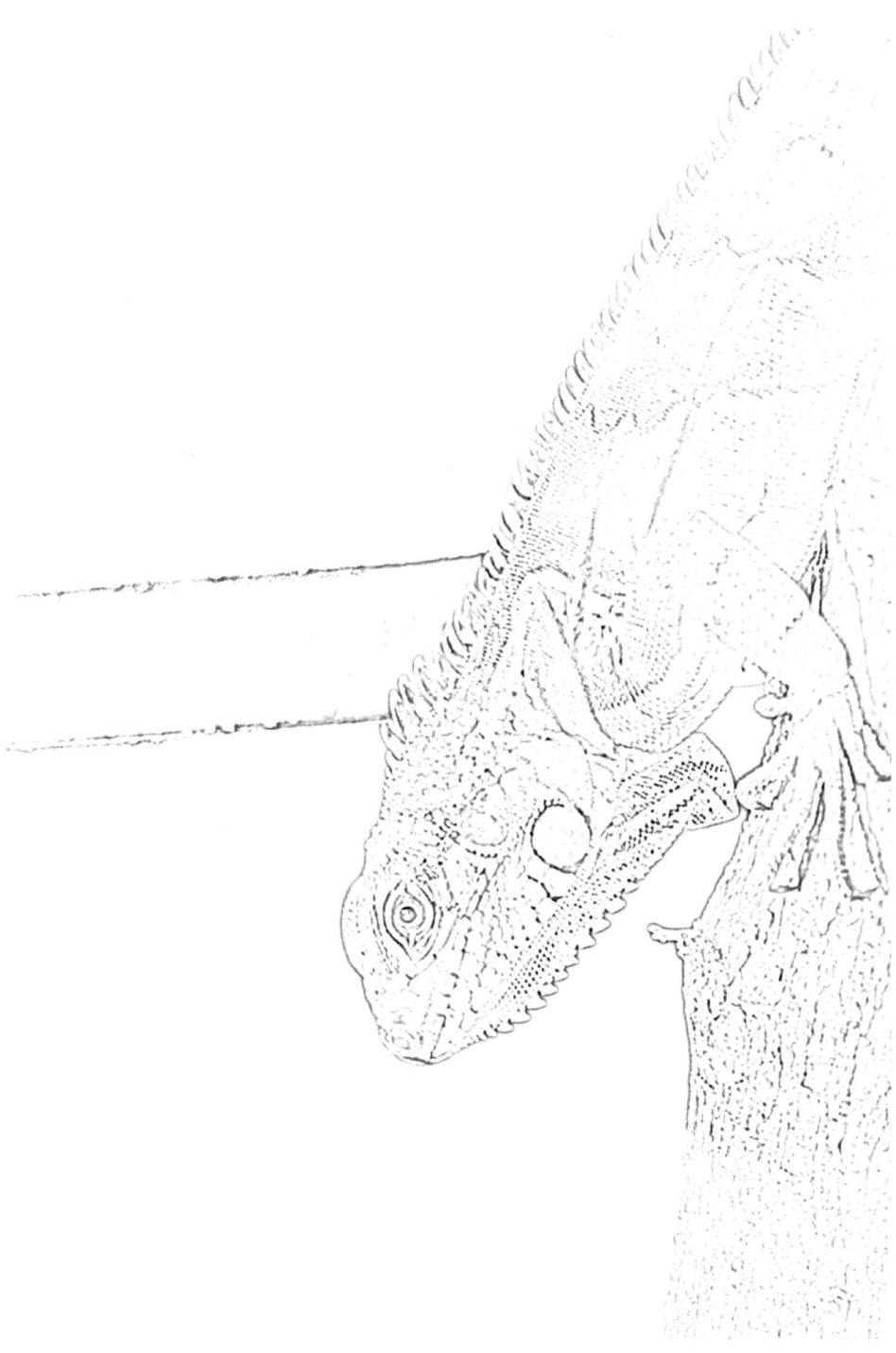

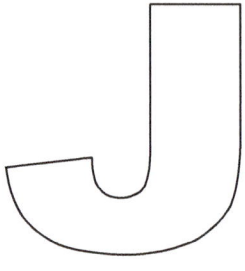

Jellyfish

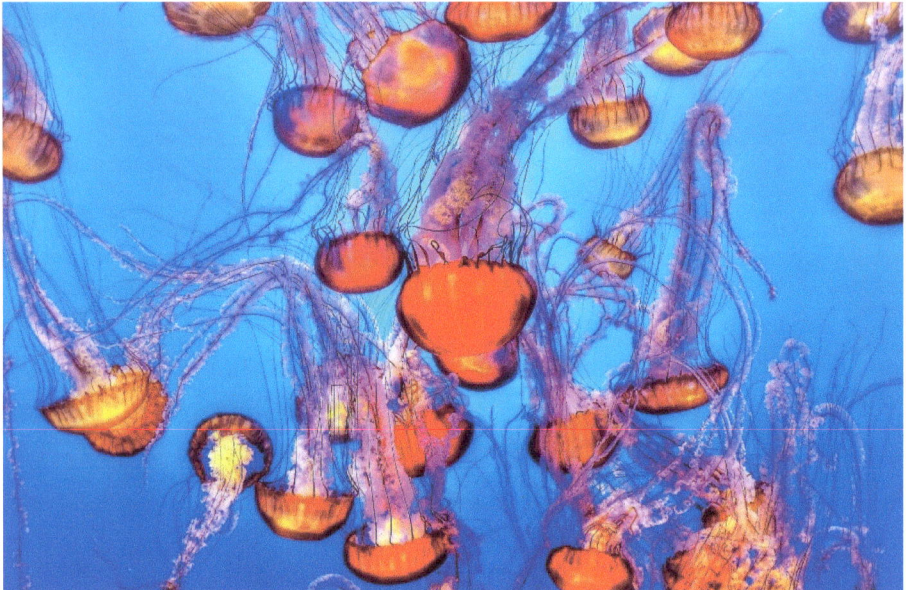

This image is of Sea Nettle which is one of the variety of jellies that sting and paralyze their prey with their tentacles.

Jellyfish are sometimes called jellies or sea jellies. But despite its name, jellyfish are not really fish at all. In fact, they are so unique to themselves that they are categorized in a class all of their own.

(Monterey Bay Aquarium, Sea Nettle, http://www.montereybayaquarium.org/animal-guide/invertebrates/sea-nettle)

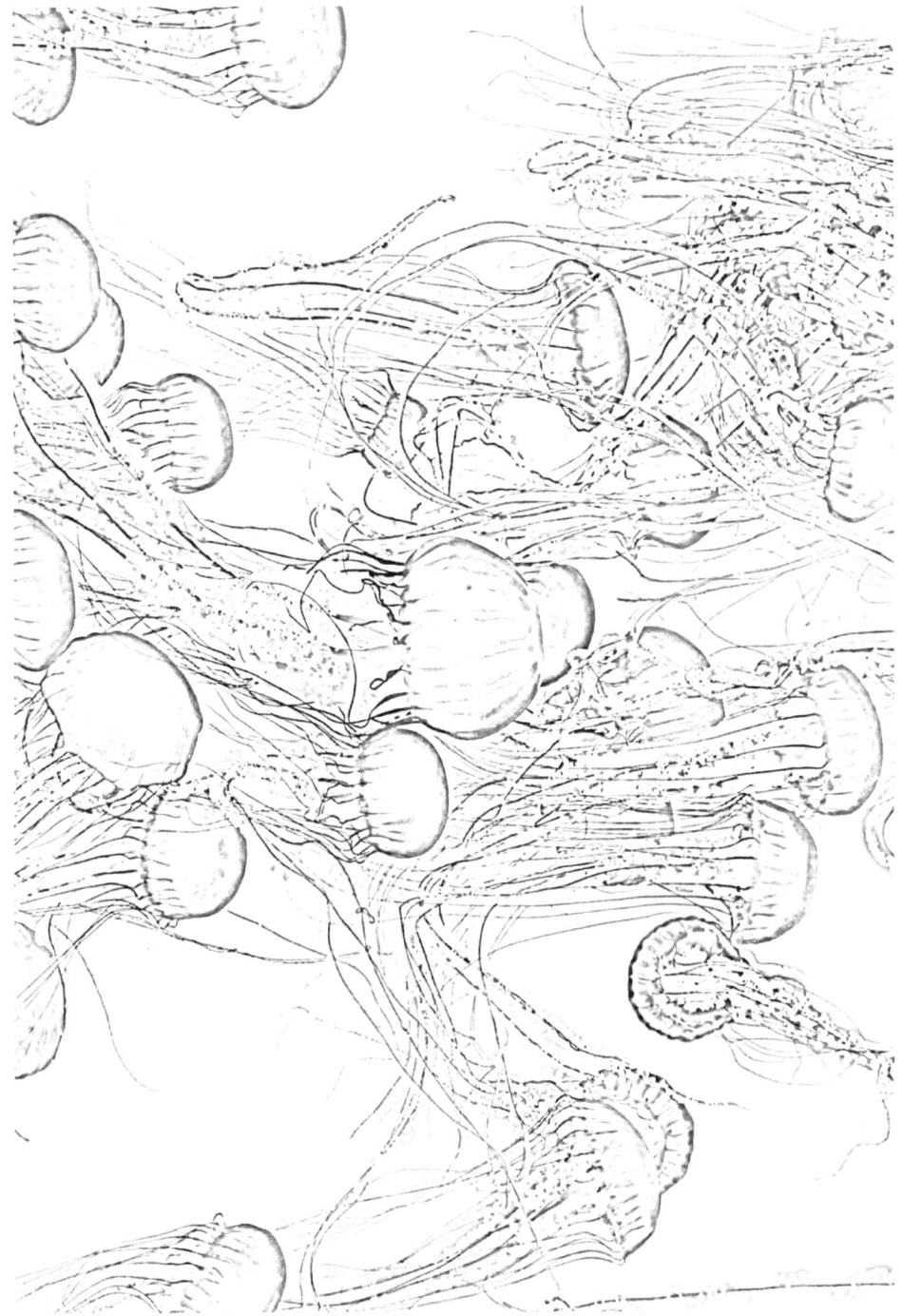

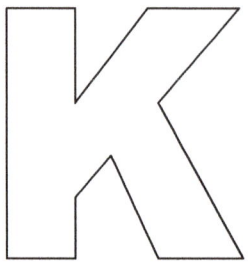

Kingfisher

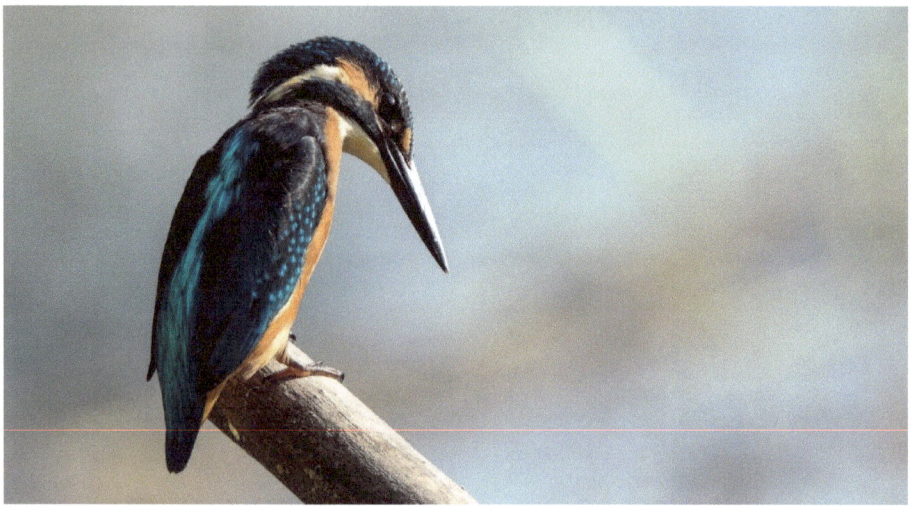

This image is most likely of a common kingfisher which is found in most of Europe, parts of Asia, and parts of North Africa.

Kingfishers are found all over the world, having more than 100 different species. There are three main types of Kingfishers though, river kingfishes, tree kingfishers, and water kingfishers.

(Beauty of Birds, Common Kingfisher, http://beautyofbirds.com/commonkingfishers.html)

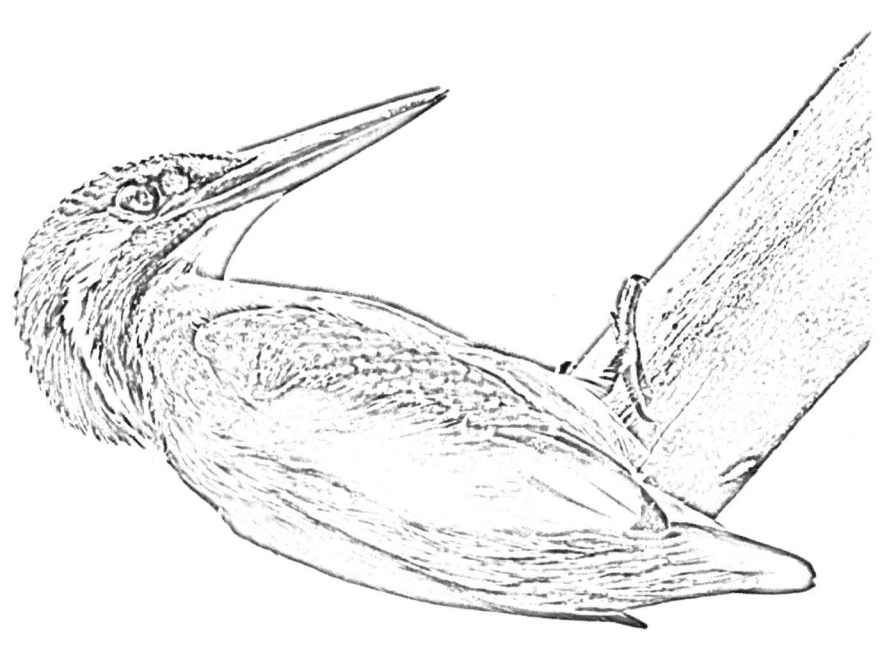

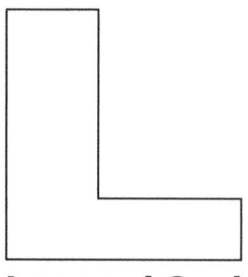

Leopard Seal

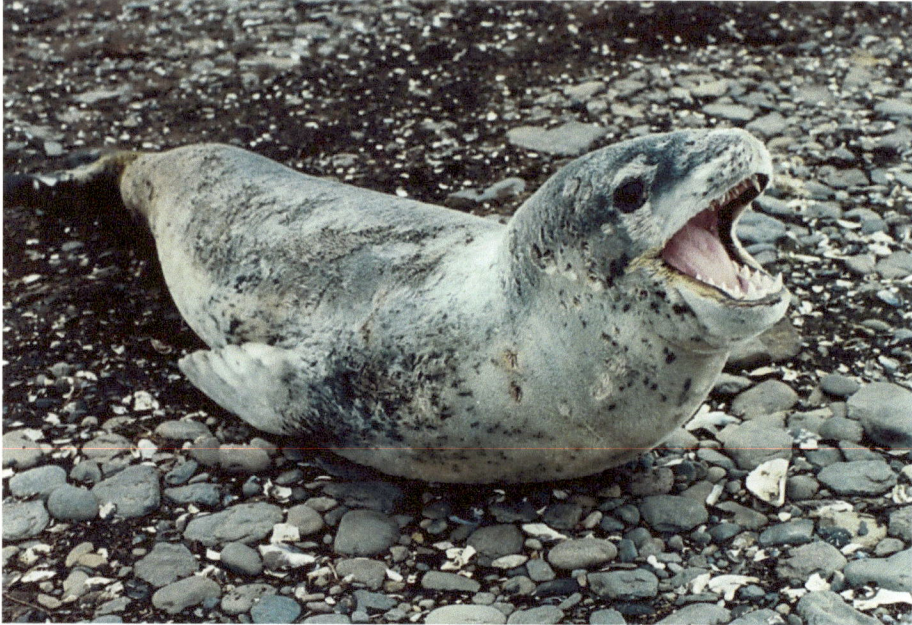

This image is of a Leopard Seal which are native to the frigid Antarctic waters, though occasionally they are found in warmer waters around South America, South Africa, New Zealand, and the southern part of Australia.

Leopard Seals are the second largest species of seal in the world and are the dominant predator in their habitats. They are rarely attacked by other animals.

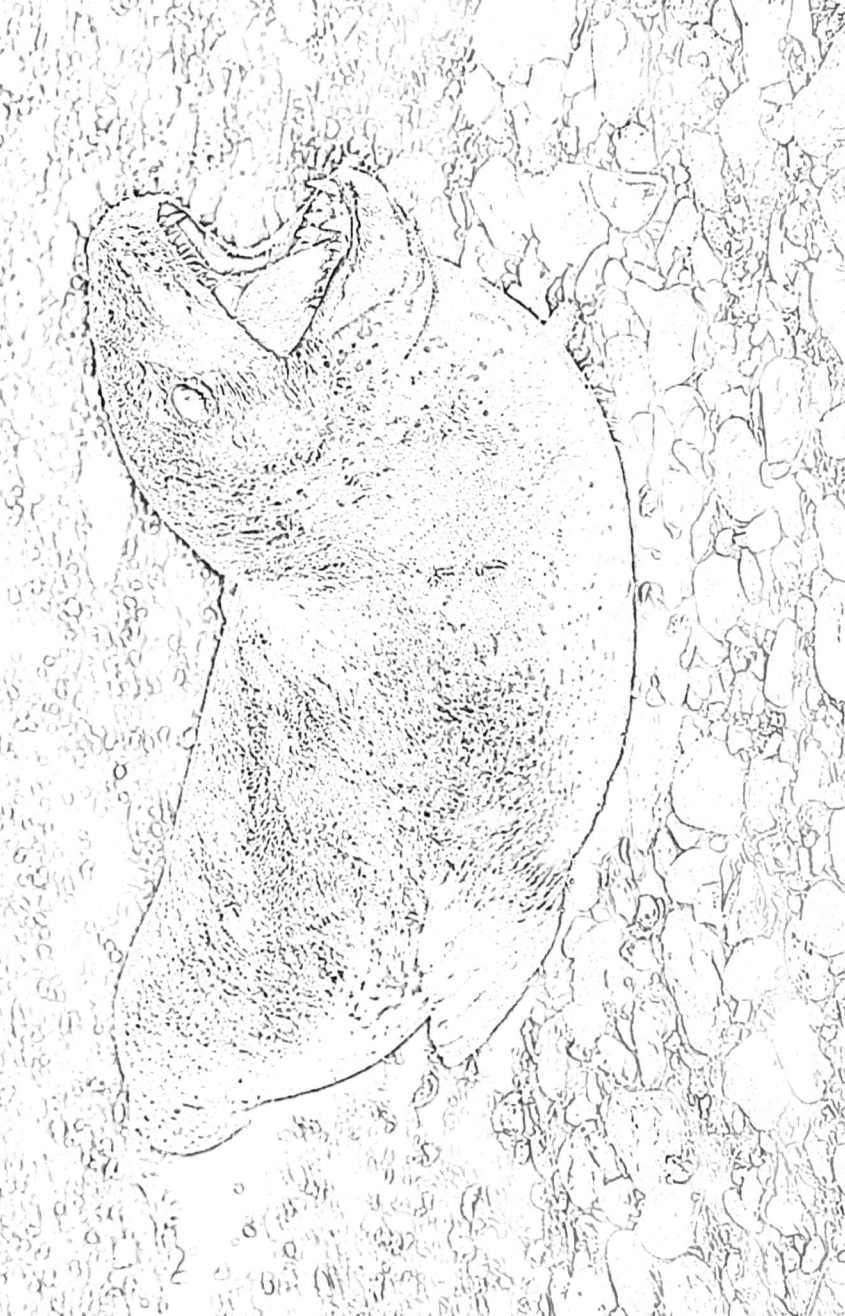

M

Macaw

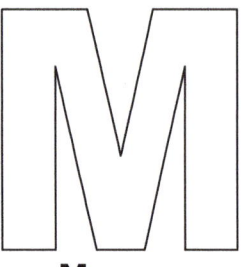

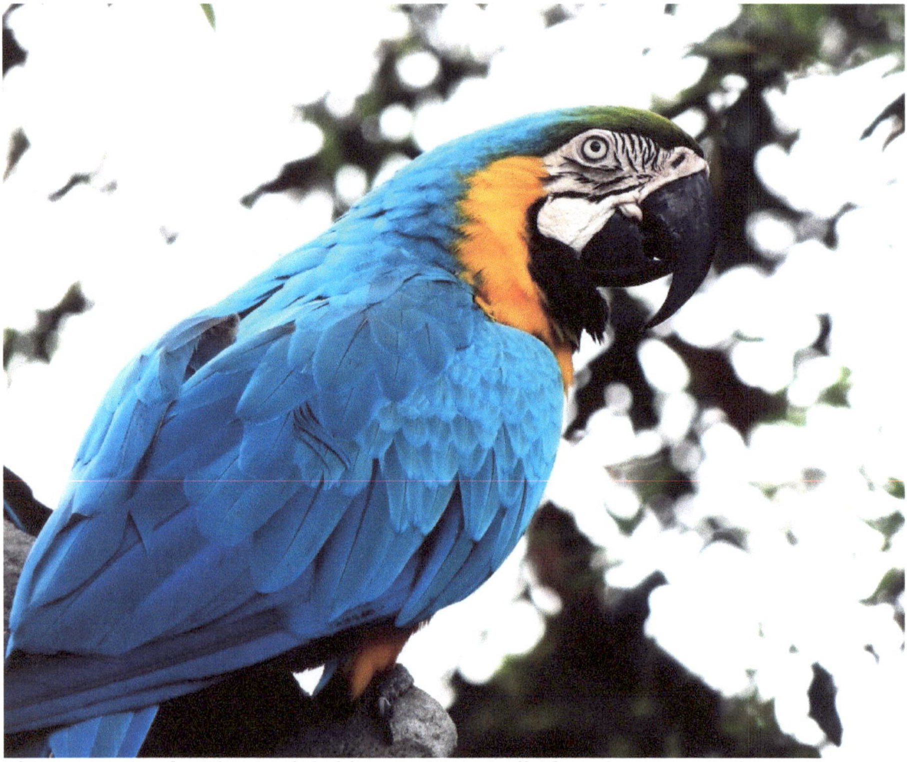

This image is of a Blue and Gold Macaw, typically found in Venezuela.

The Macaw is one of the largest species of parrots on Earth and one of the species of birds that mate for life. However, male and female macaws don't only mate for life, but they also share their food and groom one another as well.

(National Geographic, Macaw, http://animals.nationalgeographic.com/animals/birds/macaw/)

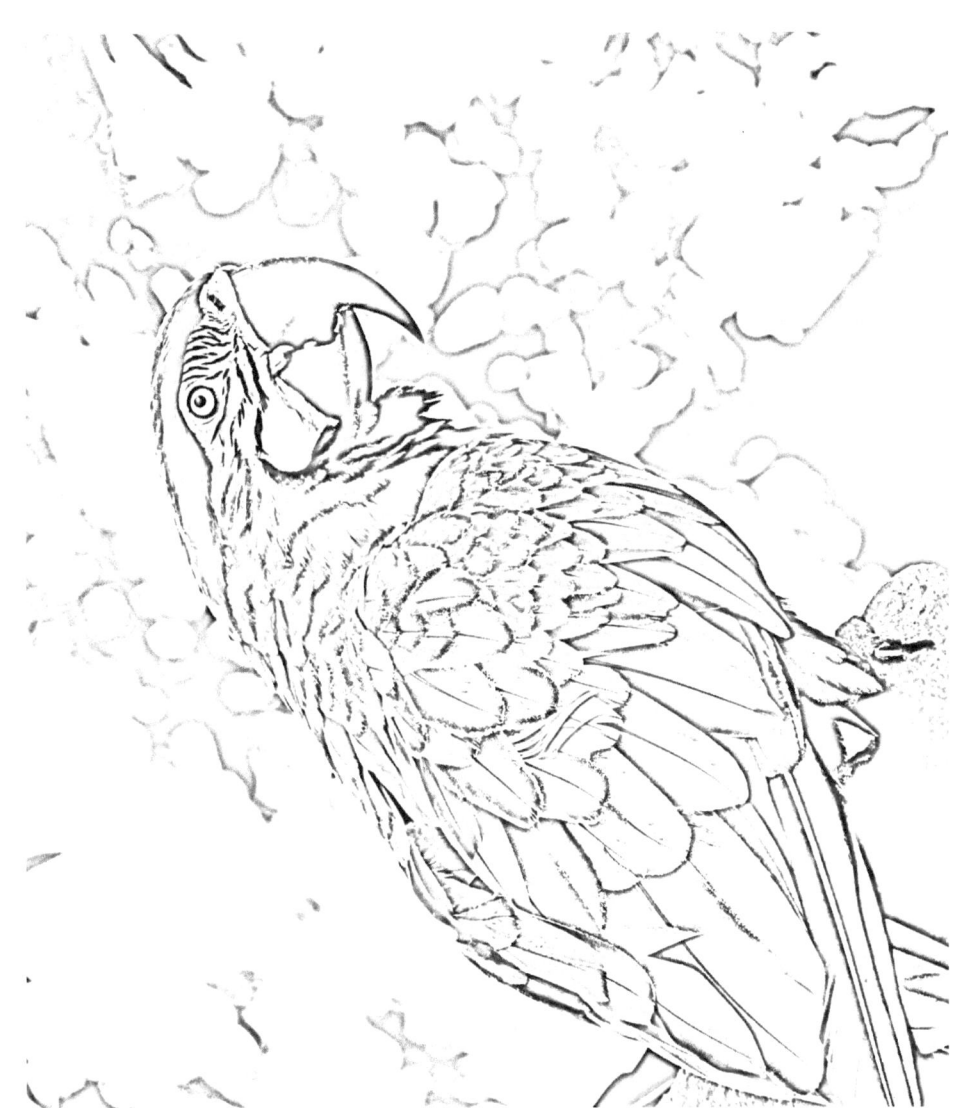

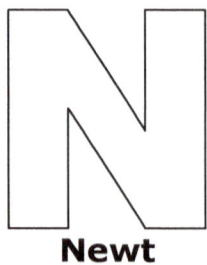

Newt

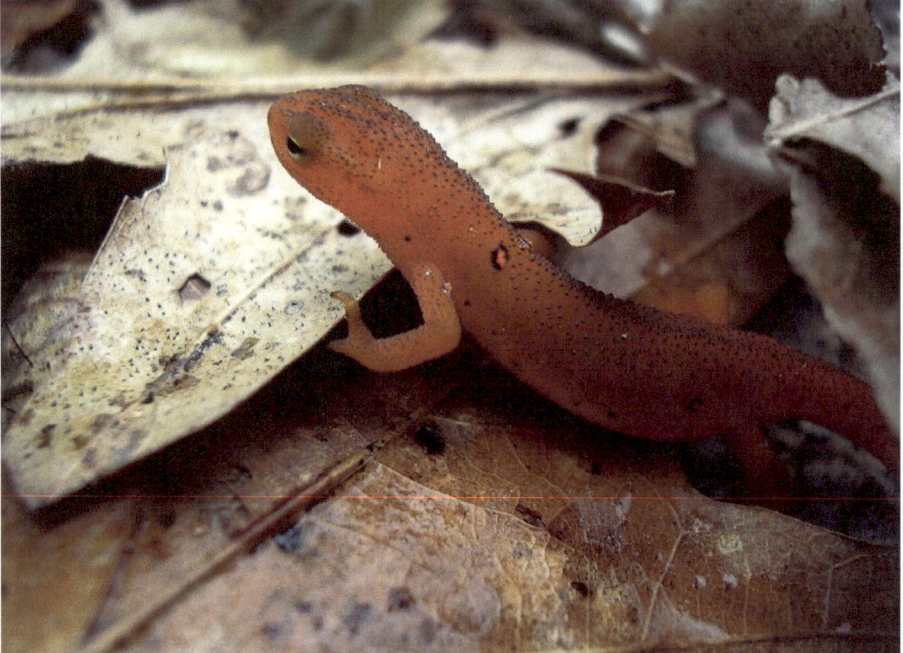

This image is of a Red Spotted Newt commonly found in West Virginia.

Newts are a subspecies of Salamanders and naturally found in North America, Europe, and Asia. Some newts have toxins that are strong enough to kill an adult human, including various species of newt native to North America. Newts can also breathe underwater and on land and are known to regrow damaged or detached limbs in a similar sense as to how other animals develop tumors.

(San Diego Zoo Animals, Salamanders and Newts, http://animals.sandiegozoo.org/animals/salamander-newt)

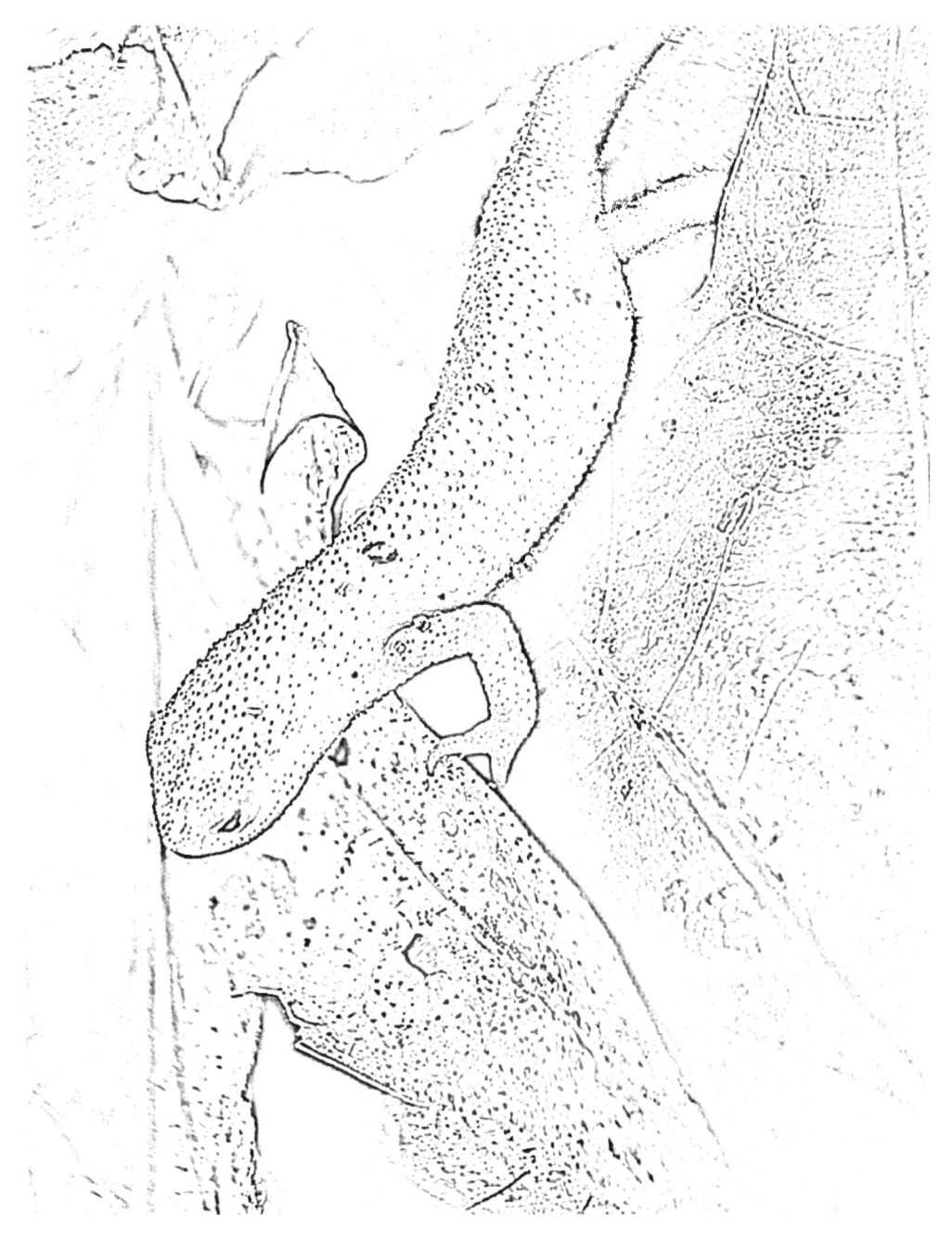

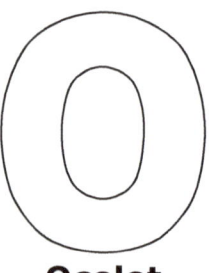

Ocelot

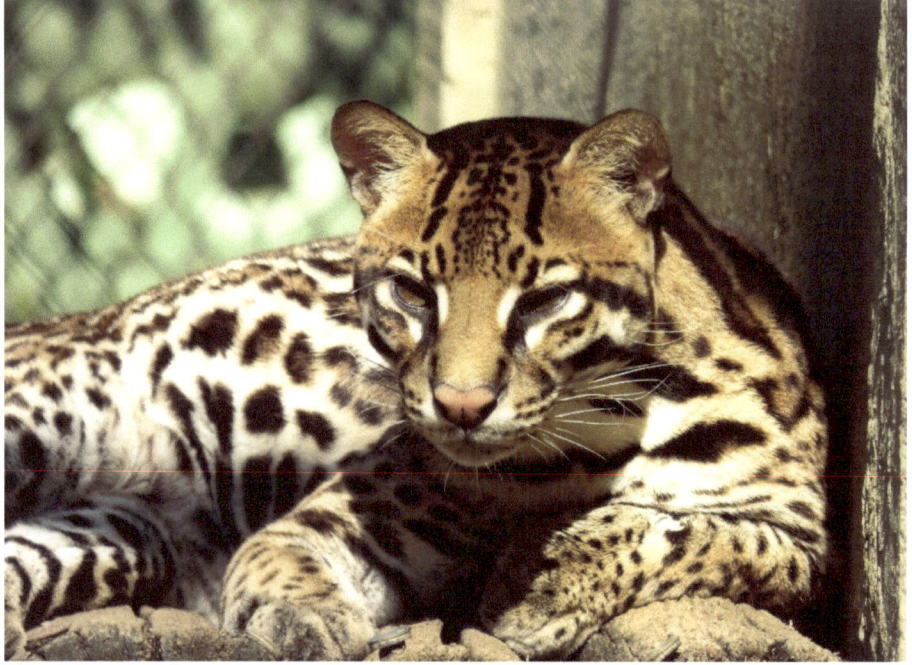

This image is of a resting Ocelot native to the jungles of South America.

The Ocelot is a medium-sized small cat that is not afraid of water. They are very agile and strong as well as both good climbers, runners, and swimmers.

(National Geographic, Ocelot,
http://animals.nationalgeographic.com/animals/mammals/ocelot/)

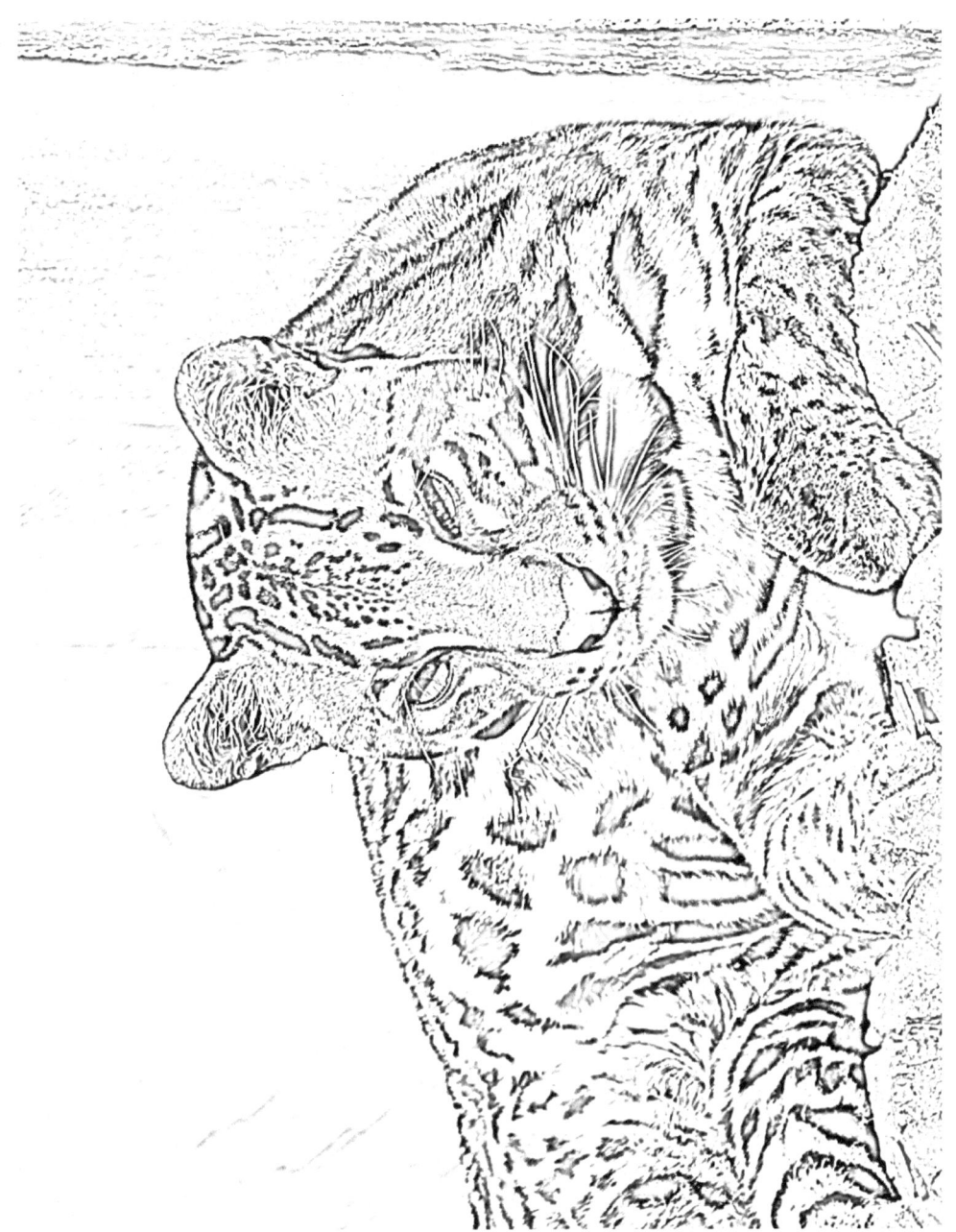

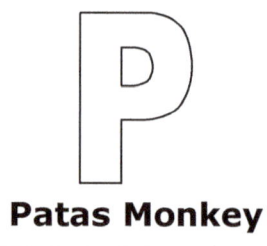

Patas Monkey

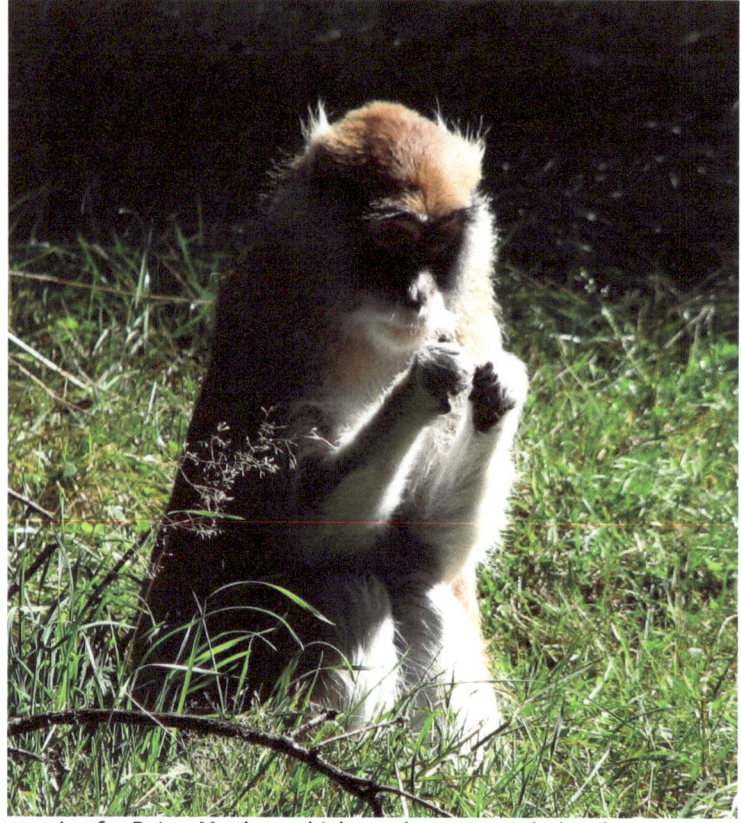

This image is of a Patas Monkey which are known to inhabit the open grasslands of Central Africa.

Known to be the fastest primates in the world, Patas Monkeys can reach speeds up to 35 mph.

(Primate Info Net, Patas Monkey, http://pin.primate.wisc.edu/factsheets/entry/patas_monkey; Image provided by "Patas.monkey3" by Mistvan - Own work. Licensed under CC BY-SA 3.0 via Wikimedia Commons - https://commons.wikimedia.org/wiki/File:Patas.monkey3.jpg#/media/File:Patas.monkey3.jpg)

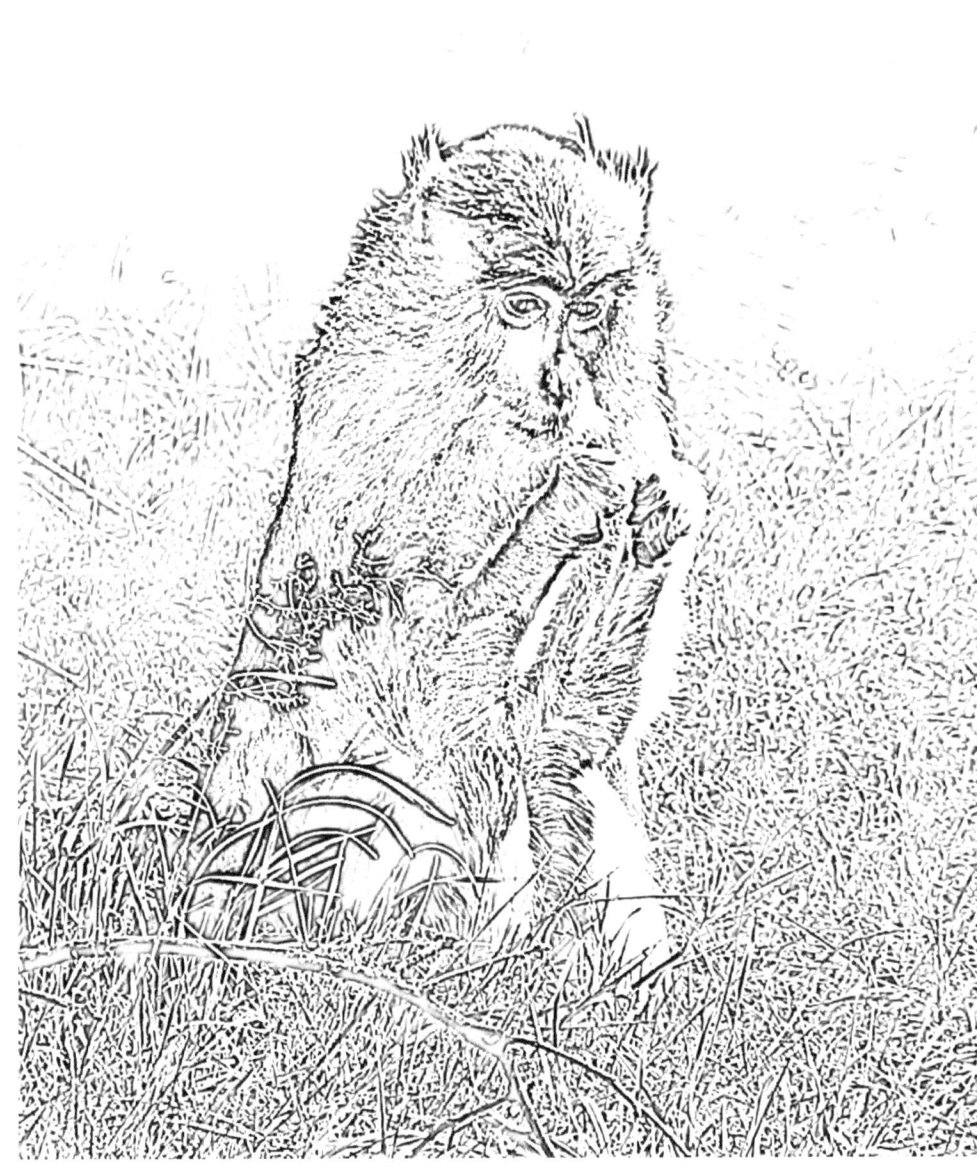

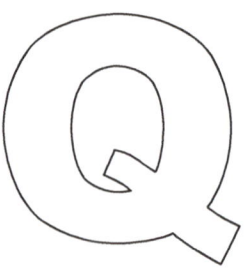

Quoll

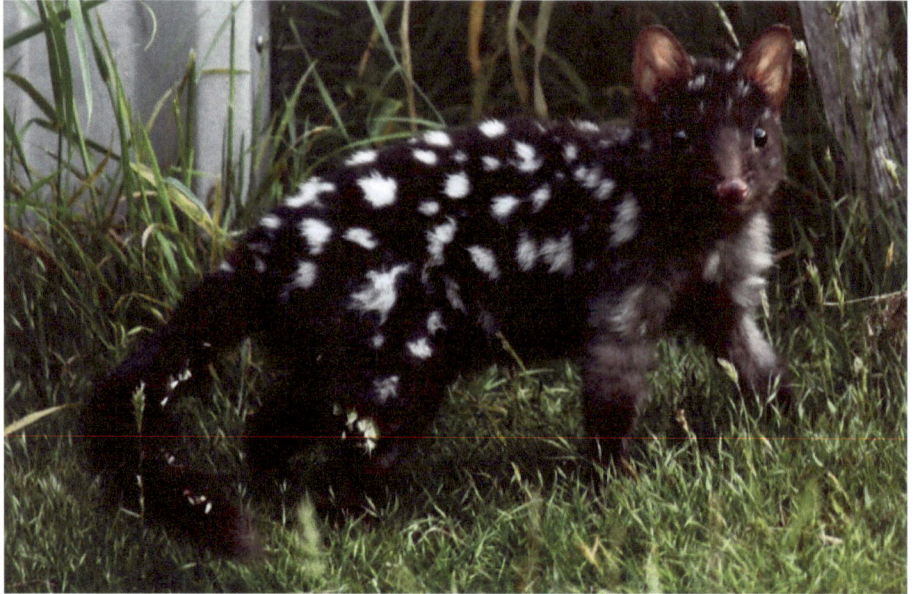

This image is of an Eastern Black Quoll found in Northern or Eastern Tasmania.

Quolls are medium-sized marsupials (meaning the females have a pouch on their stomachs where their young develop, such as with kangaroos). The quoll is a nocturnal animal that enjoys basking in the sunlight during the daylight hours. Their main predators consist mostly of humans, large snakes, and crocodiles.

(Australian Quoll Conservancy, http://www.quolls.org.au/; Image provided by "Eastern Quoll (Black)" by Ways - Own work. Licensed under CC BY-SA 3.0 via Wikimedia Commons - https://commons.wikimedia.org/wiki/File:Eastern_Quoll_(Black).jpg#/media/File:Eastern_Quoll_(Black).jpg)

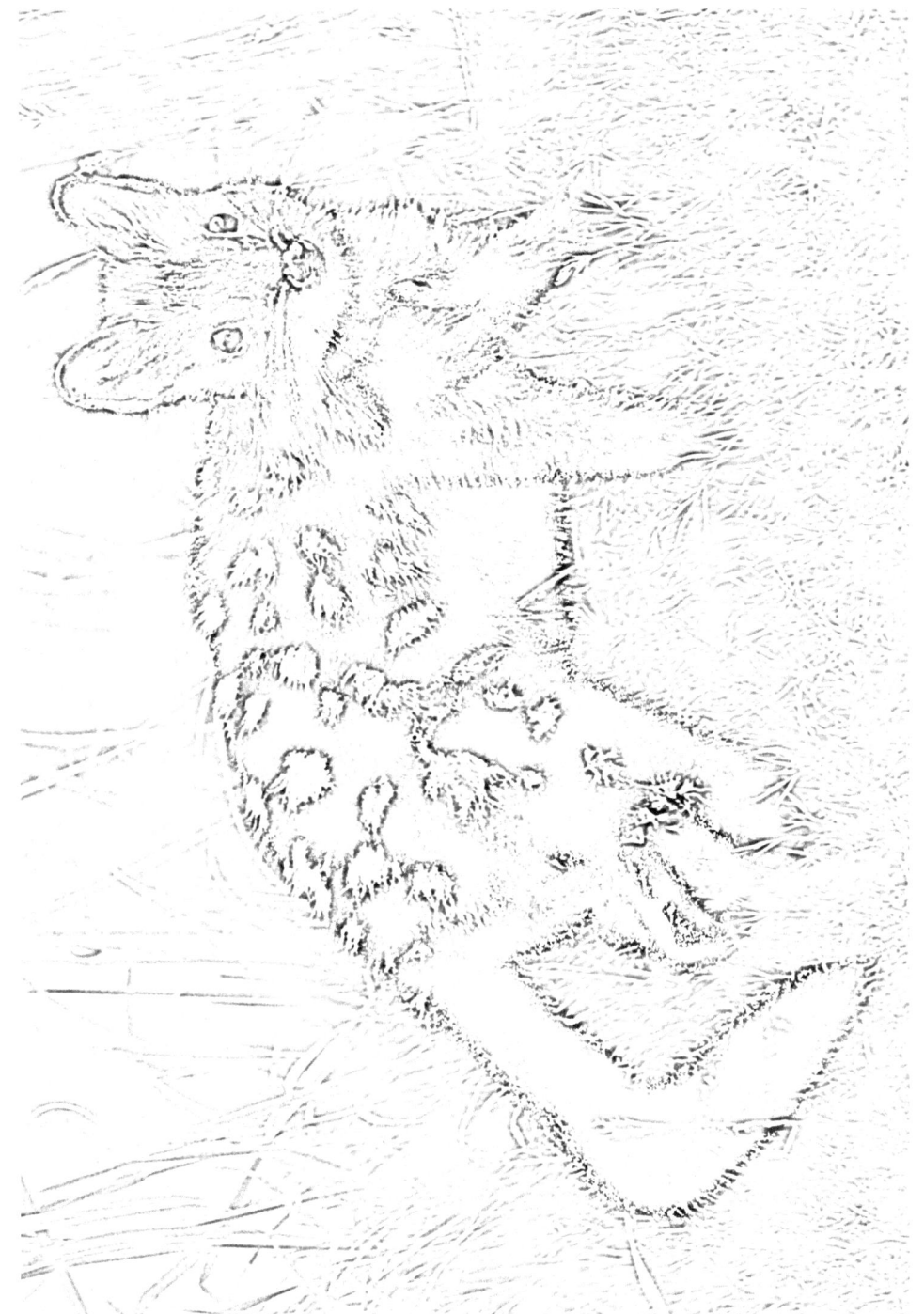

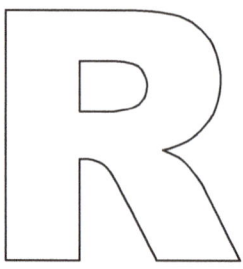

Red Panda

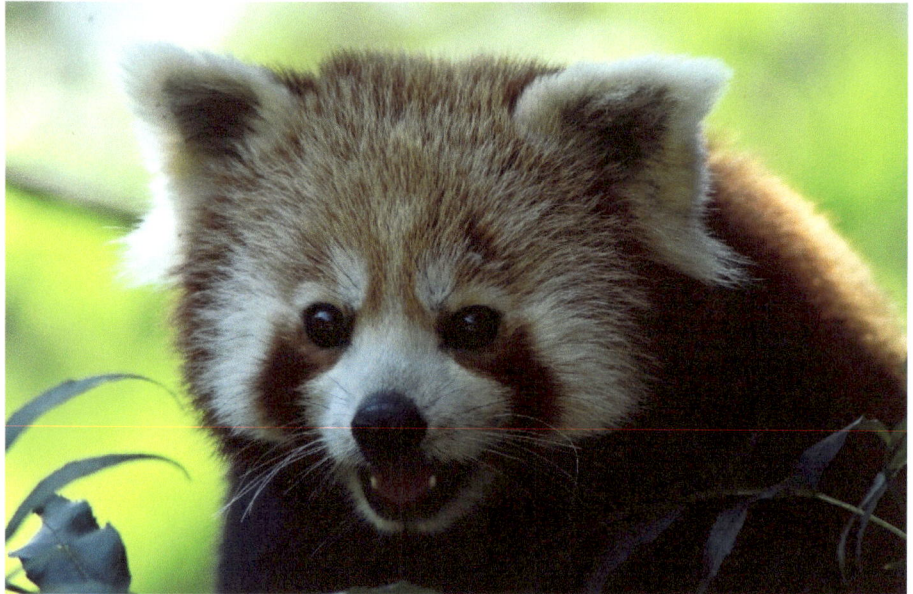

This image is of a Red Panda which are native to the temperate forests of the Himalayas.

The Red Panda is a cat-sized carnivorous creature that relies heavily on bamboo, much like its relative, the Giant Panda. Because of this, even though these mammals are carnivorous, they tend to lead very vegetarian diets.

(National Geographic, Red Panda, http://animals.nationalgeographic.com/animals/mammals/red-panda/)

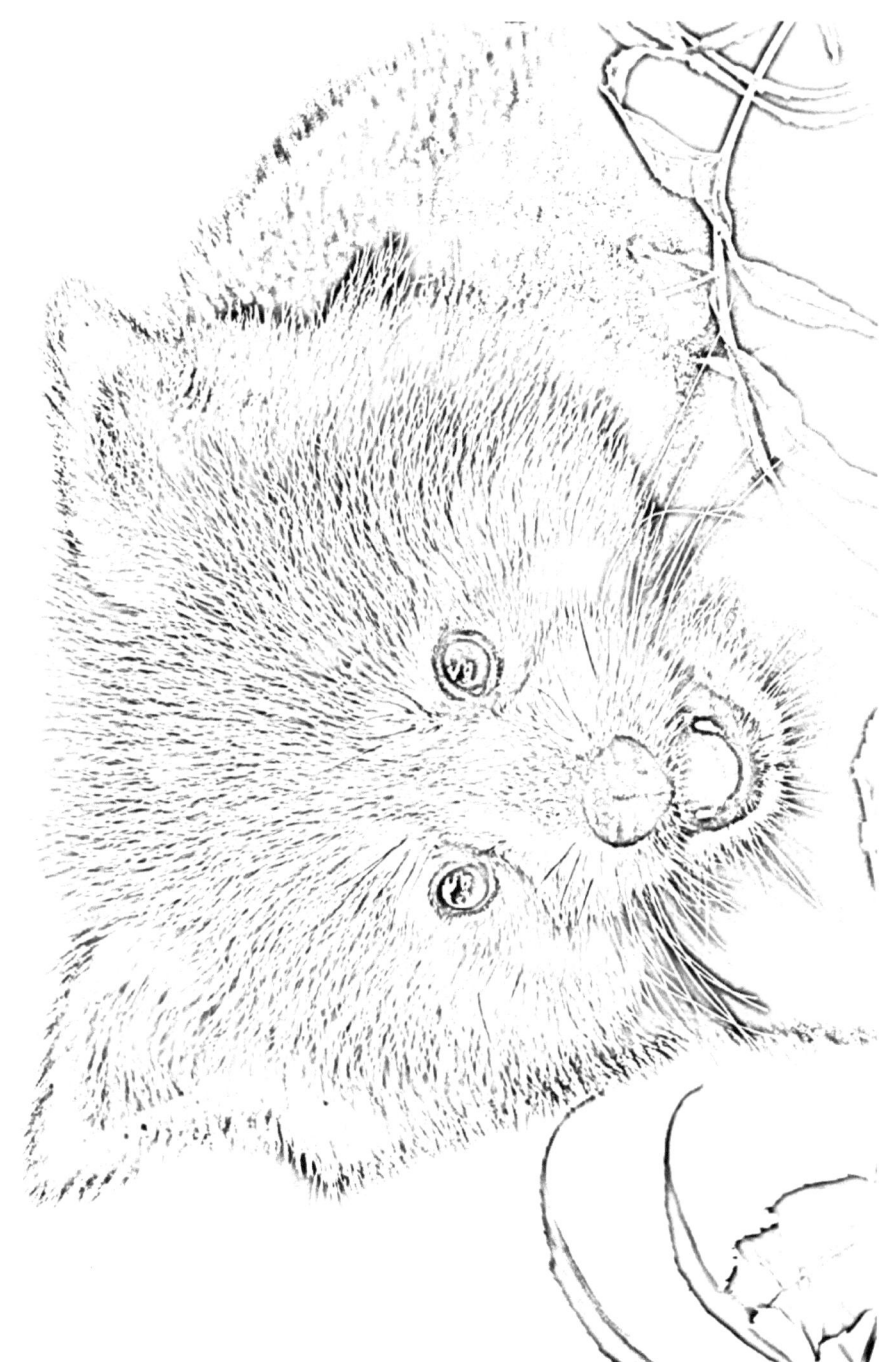

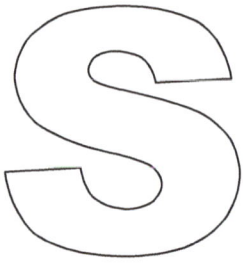

Sea Dragon

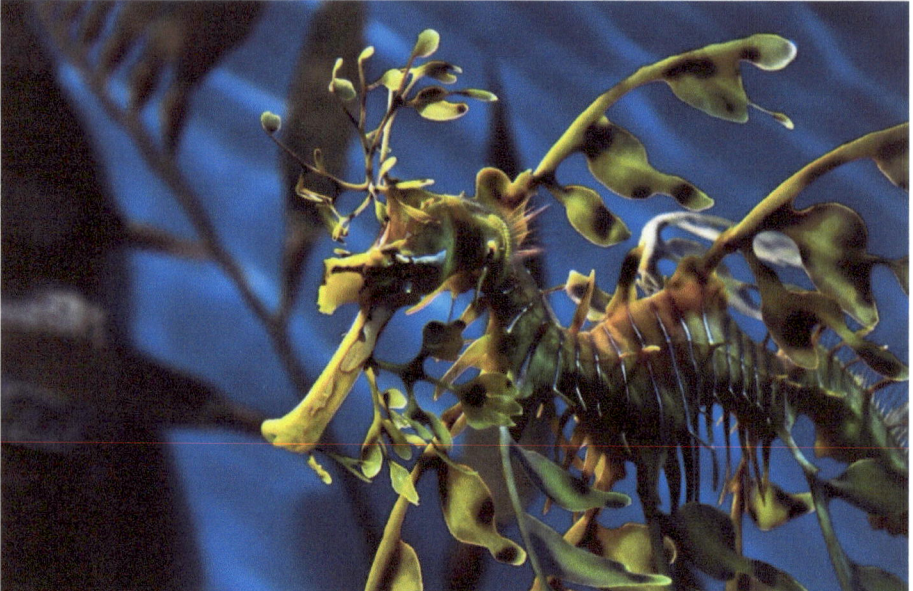

This image is of a Leafy Sea Dragon, native only to the tropical coastal waters of south and west Australia.

Sea Dragons are small, carnivorous fish subsisting entirely off meat. They typically will hunt crustaceans, plankton, shrimp, and even other small fish. They are closely related to seahorses.

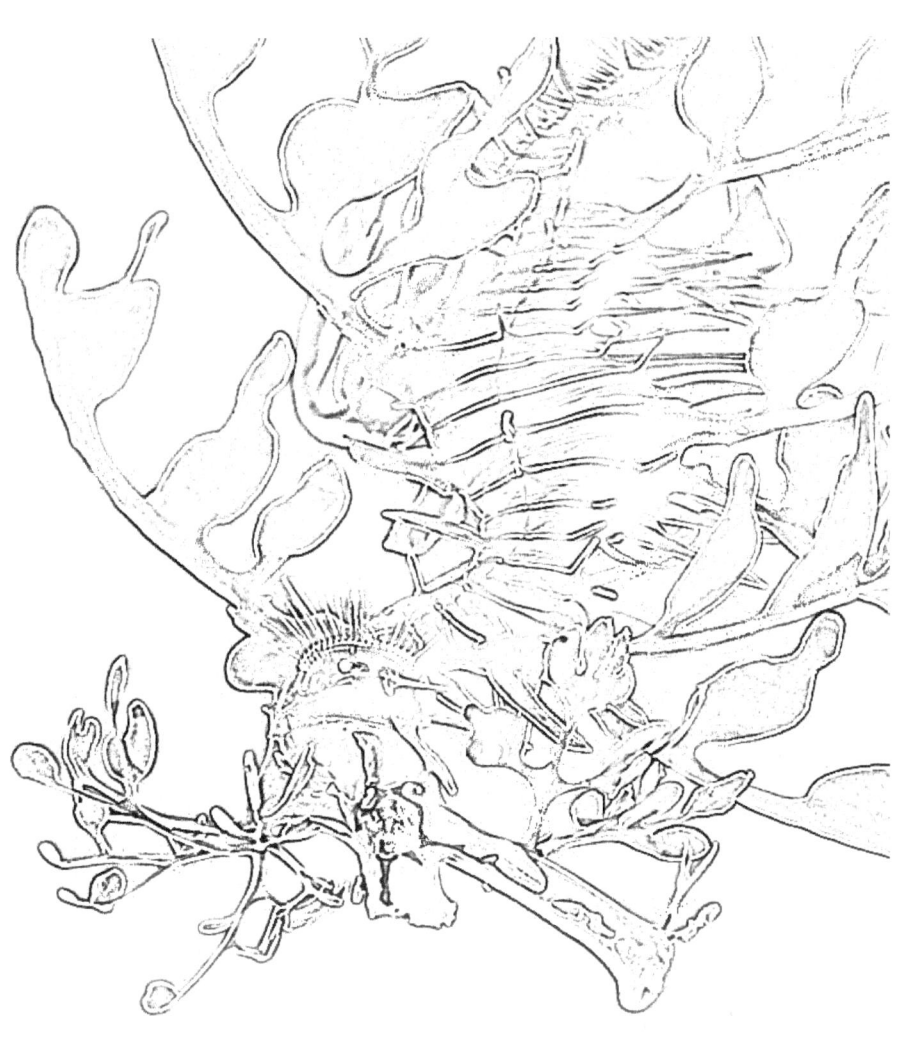

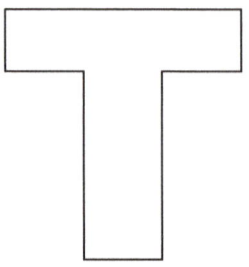

Toucan

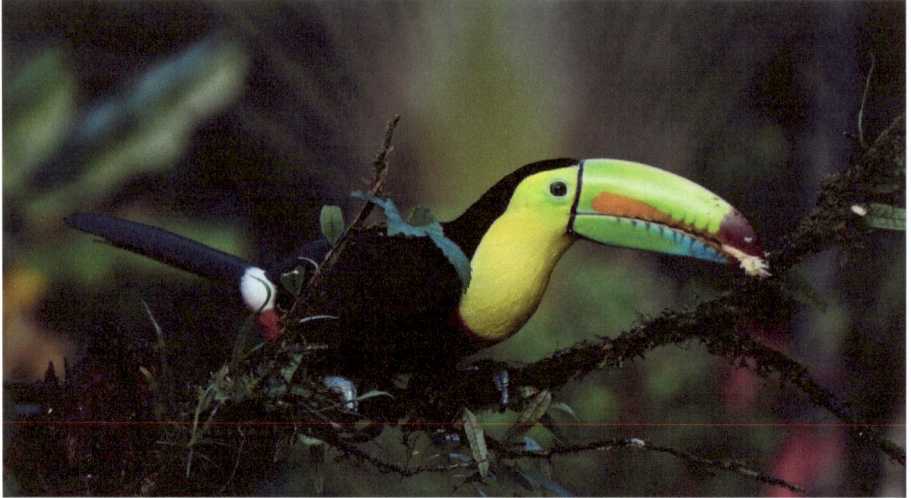

This image is of a Keel Billed Toucan most likely found in Costa Rica.

Toucans are best known for their colorful beaks, which are surprisingly light as they are made up entirely out of keratin (the same substance that is used to form our nails and hair, as well as many other animals' nails and hair). It is used mostly for intimidation purposes and not for defense.

(Neotropical Birds, Keel-billed Toucan, http://neotropical.birds.cornell.edu/portal/species/lifehistory?p_p_spp=303256)

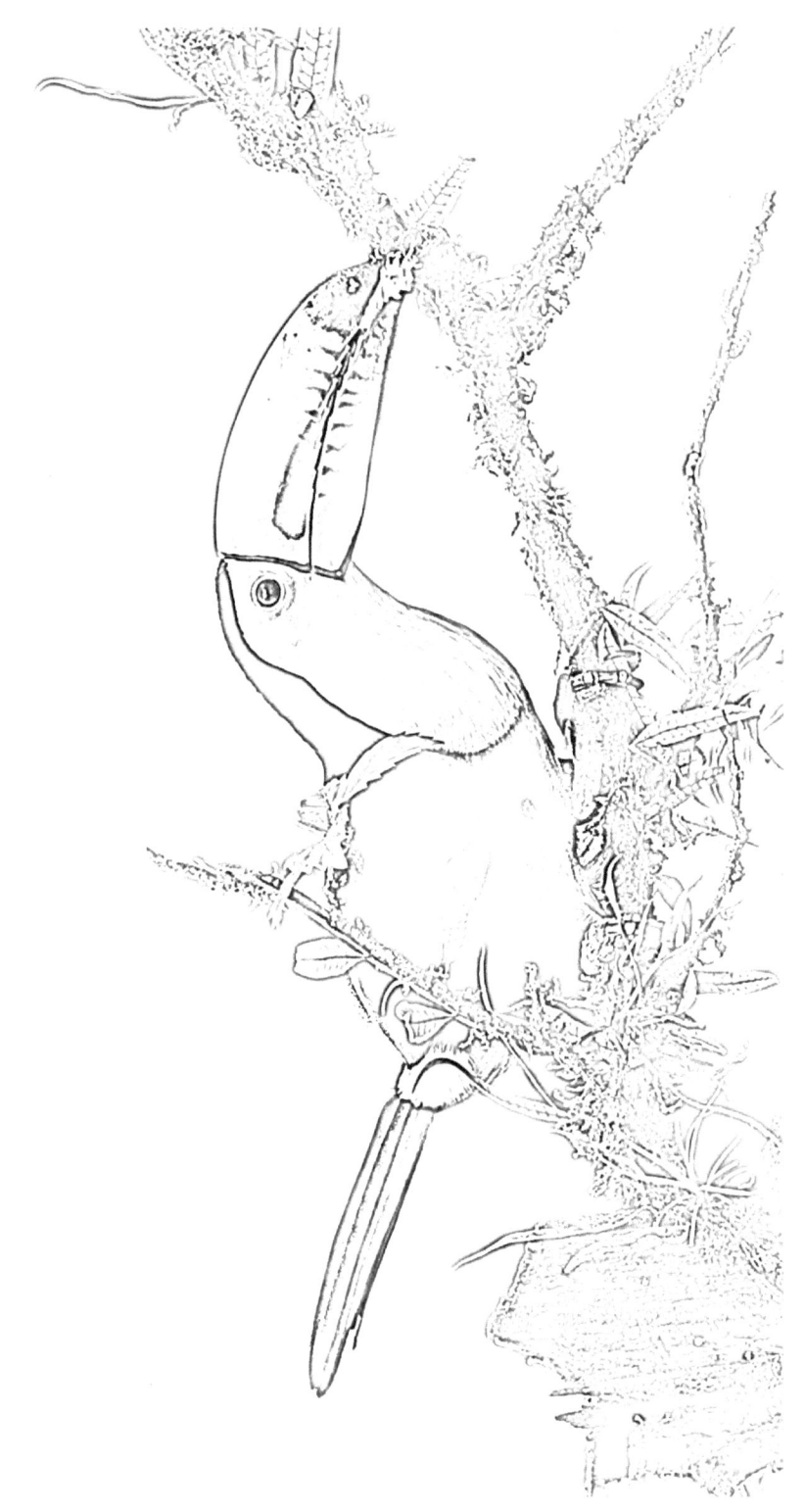

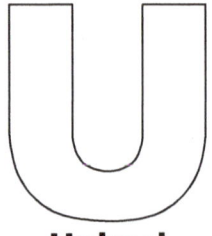

Uakari

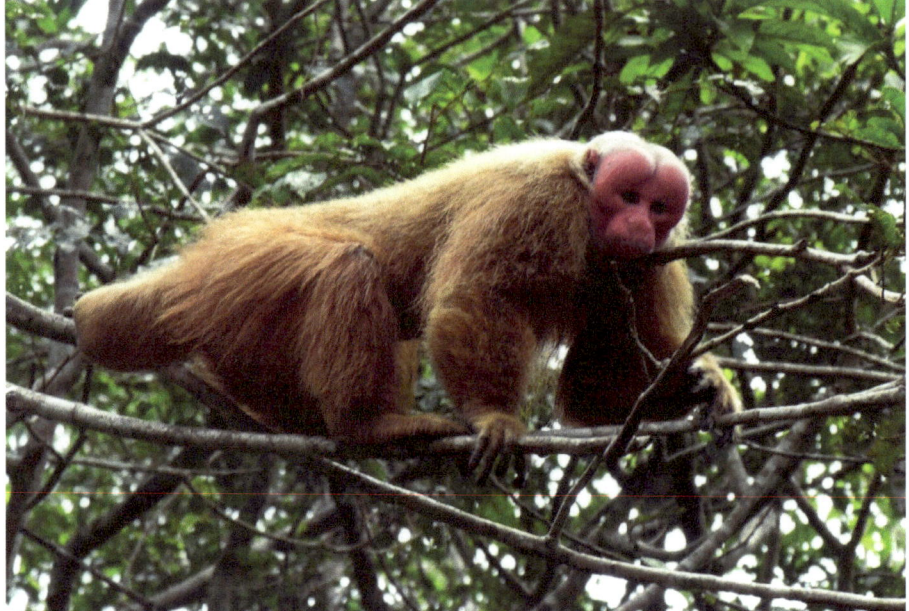

This image is of a Uakari which are typically found in the tropical rainforests of South America, close to water.

The Uakari (pronounced "wakari") is a small species of monkey known mostly for its naked face that typically ranges in coloration between pink and deep red. The depth of color in their faces can actually help to determine the health of the individual, as sick or captive Uakari tend to have noticeably paler skin than those that are healthy and in the wild.

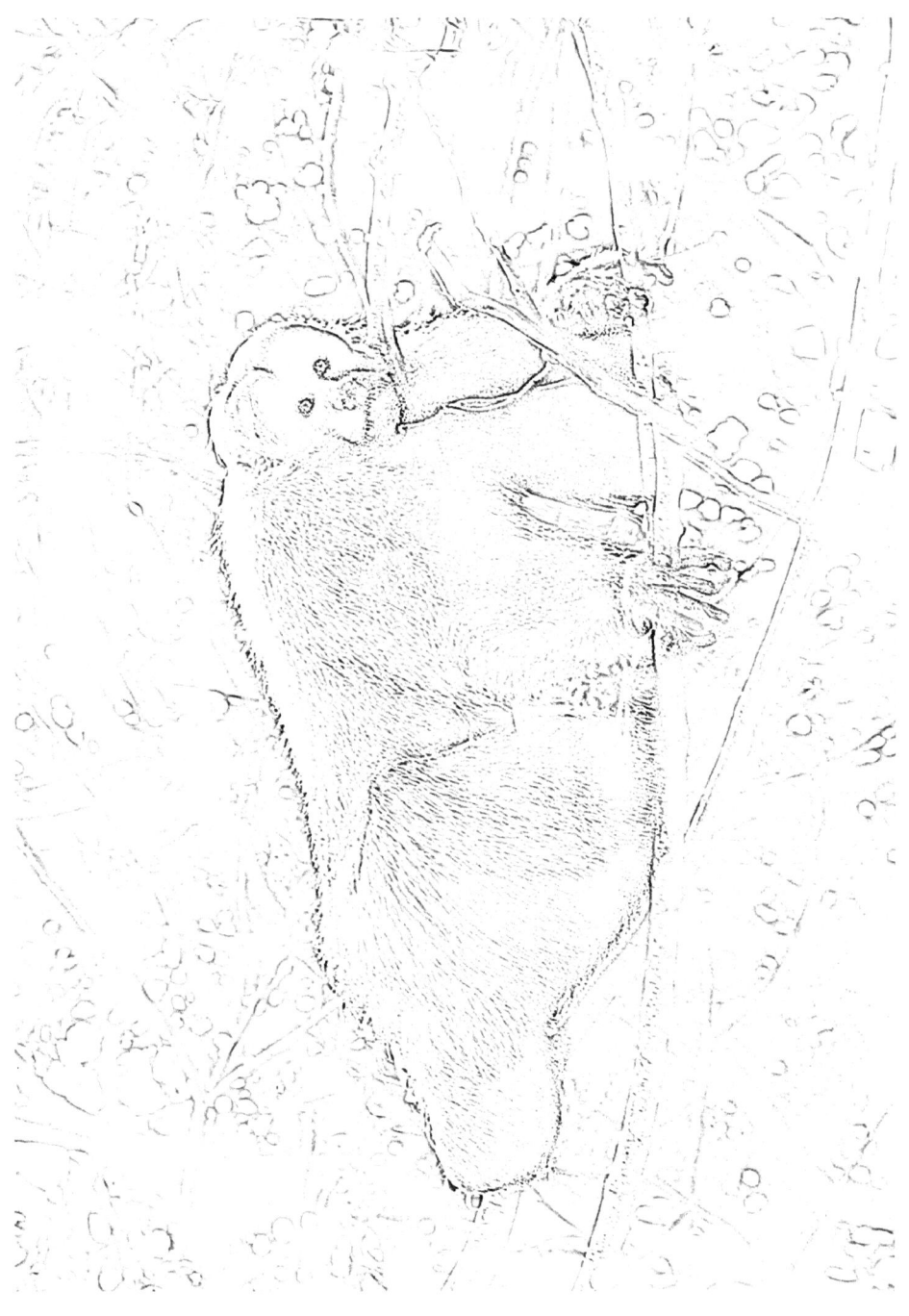

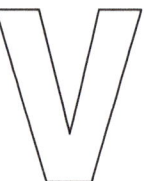

Vulture

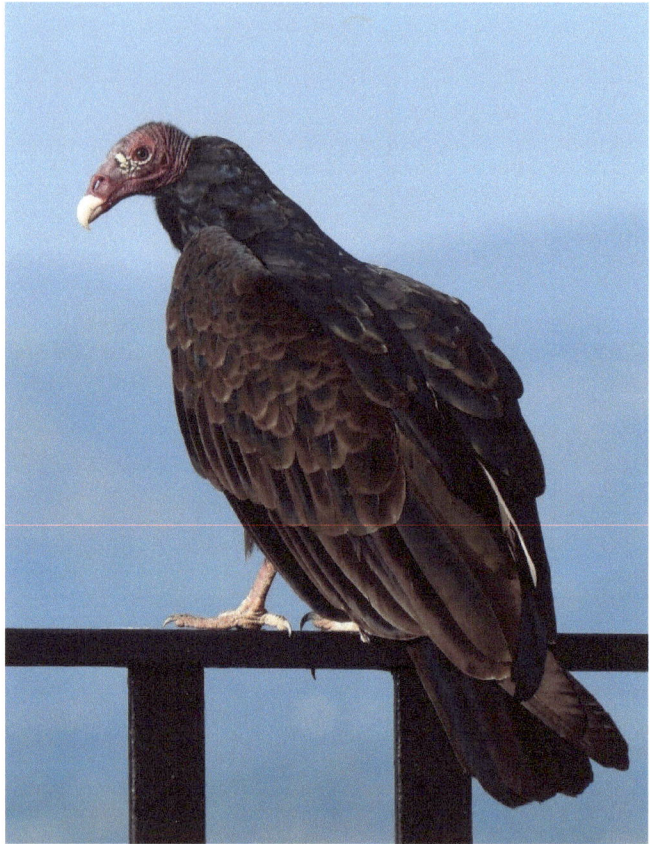

This image is of a Turkey Vulture common to North and South America.

Vultures are found on every continent except for Australia and Antarctica. There are two main types of vultures known as Old World Vultures and New World Vultures. Old World Vultures are found in Europe, Asia, and Africa and are thought to be most commonly related to eagles and hawks, whereas New World Vultures can be found in the Americas. These two types of vultures are not closely linked via DNA, despite their similarities, but rather through evolutionary status.

(All About Birds, Turkey Vulture,
https://www.allaboutbirds.org/guide/Turkey_Vulture/id)

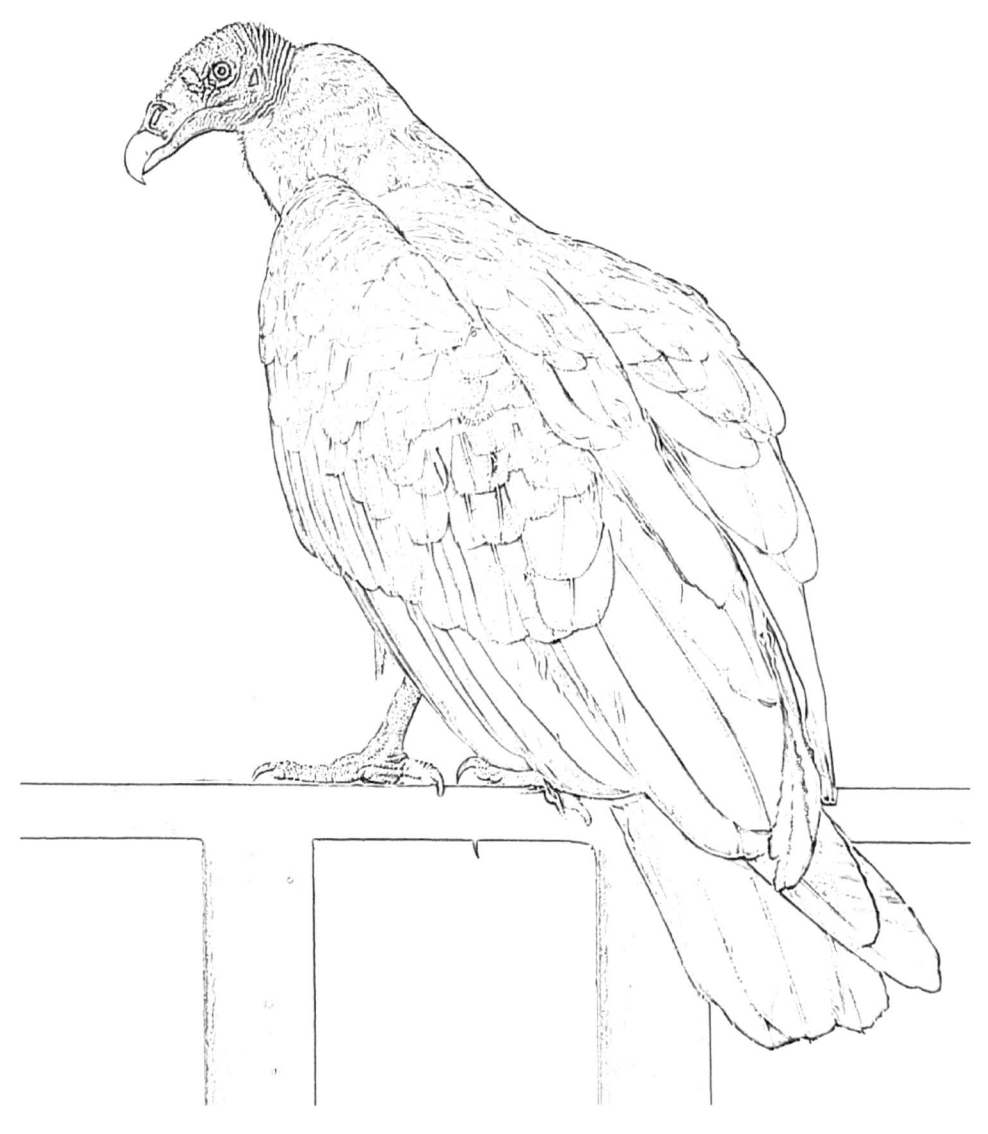

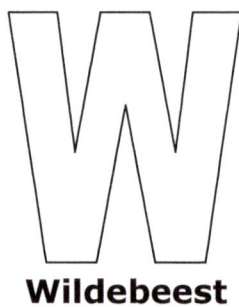

Wildebeest

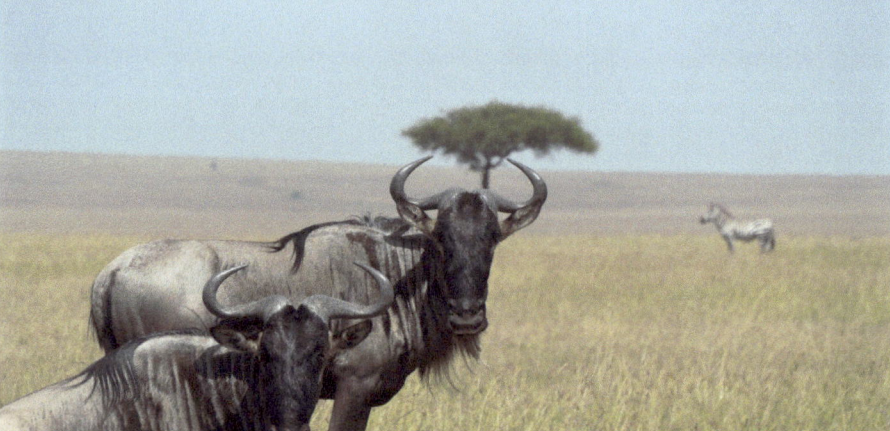

This image is of a pair of Wildebeest common to most of Africa.

Despite their bull-like appearance, the Wildebeest are actually a sub-species of antelope. The wildebeest survive mainly off of grass and therefore are forced to migrate during the dry months. Incredibly, wildebeest can sense thunderstorms up to 30 miles away and are known to follow in their path, which has come to be known as the Great Migration.

(African Wildlife Foundation, Wildebeest, http://www.awf.org/wildlife-conservation/wildebeest)

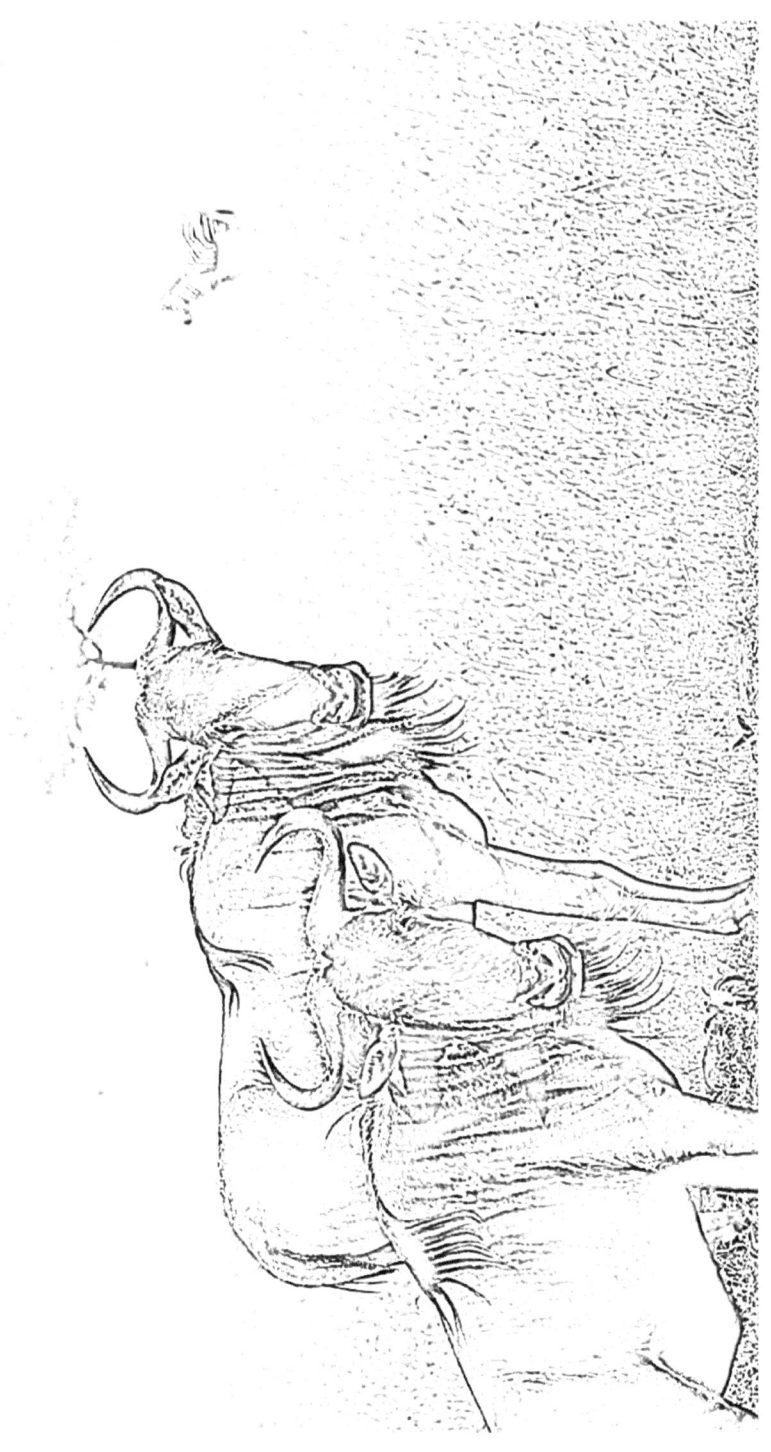

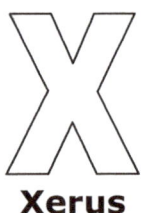

Xerus

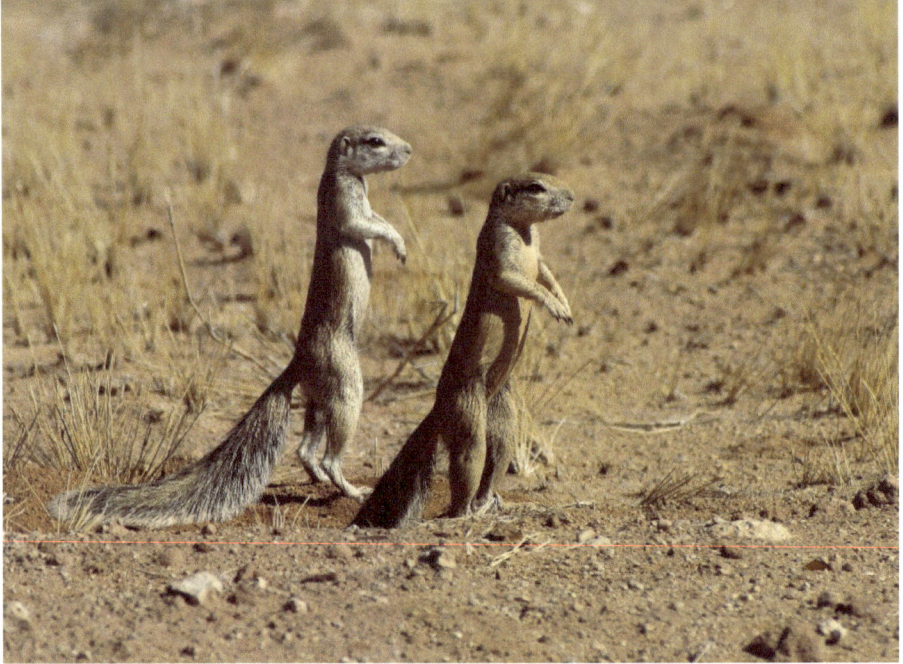

This image is of two Xerus commonly found in South Africa.

Xerus, also known as the South African Ground Squirrel, are common to most of Southern Africa including Namibia, Botswana, South Africa, and parts of the Kalahari Desert. Their known predators include the black backed jackal, which xerus will hide from for prolonged periods of time if present. Xerus help provide crucial habitat and protection for other species including meerkats and yellow mongooses.

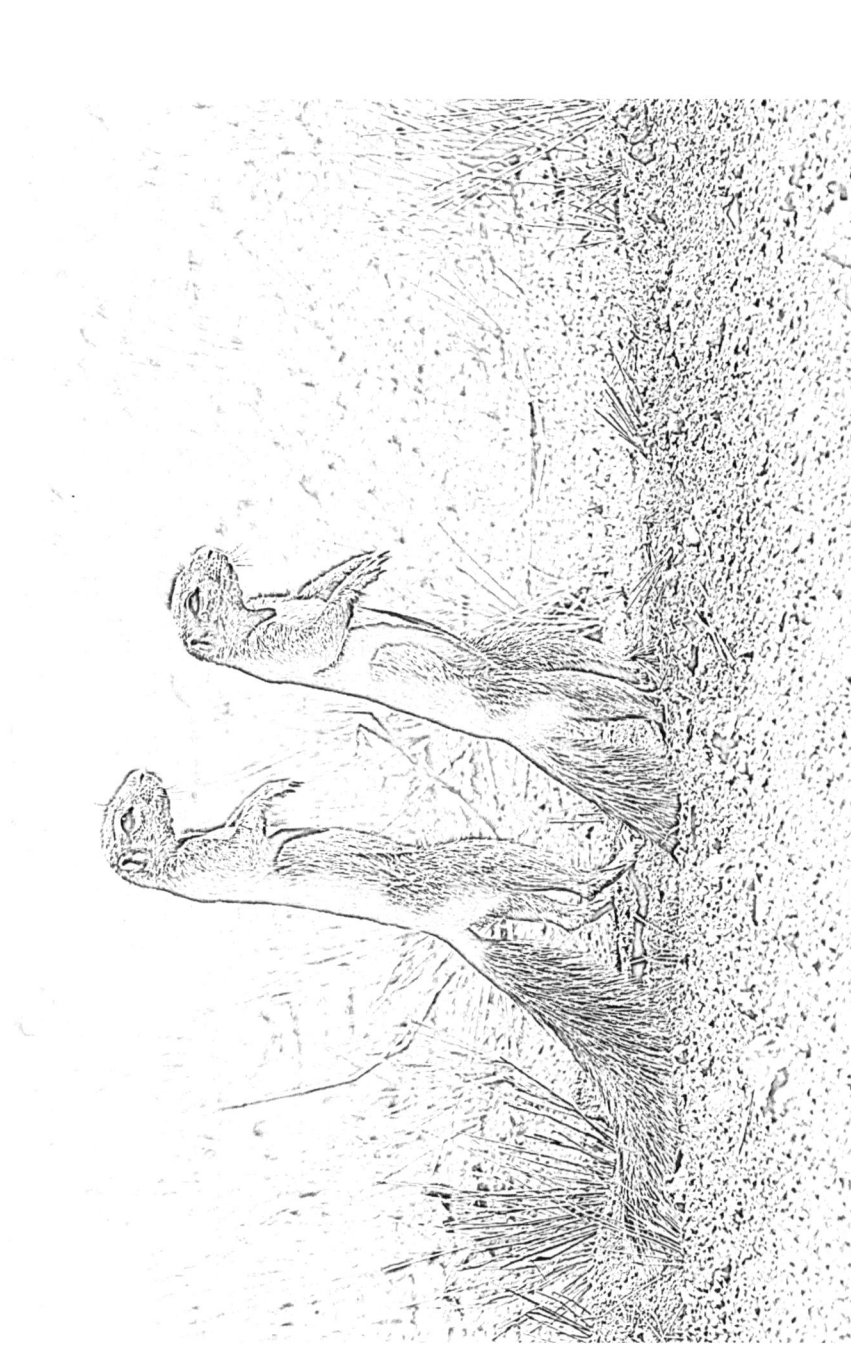

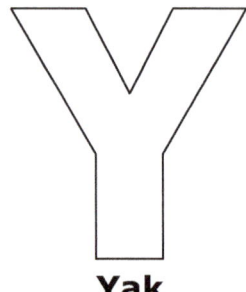

Yak

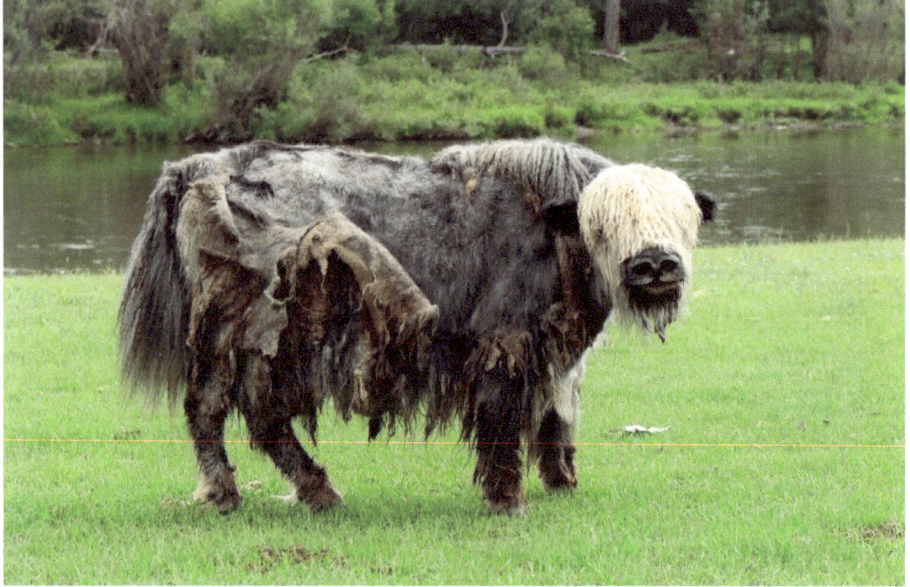

This image is of a wild Yak found in Mongolia.

Yaks use their horns to break through the snow in order to reach the plants that are buried beneath it. They will also use their horns defensively when necessary.

(Animal Info, Yak, http://www.animalinfo.org/species/artiperi/bos_mutu.htm)

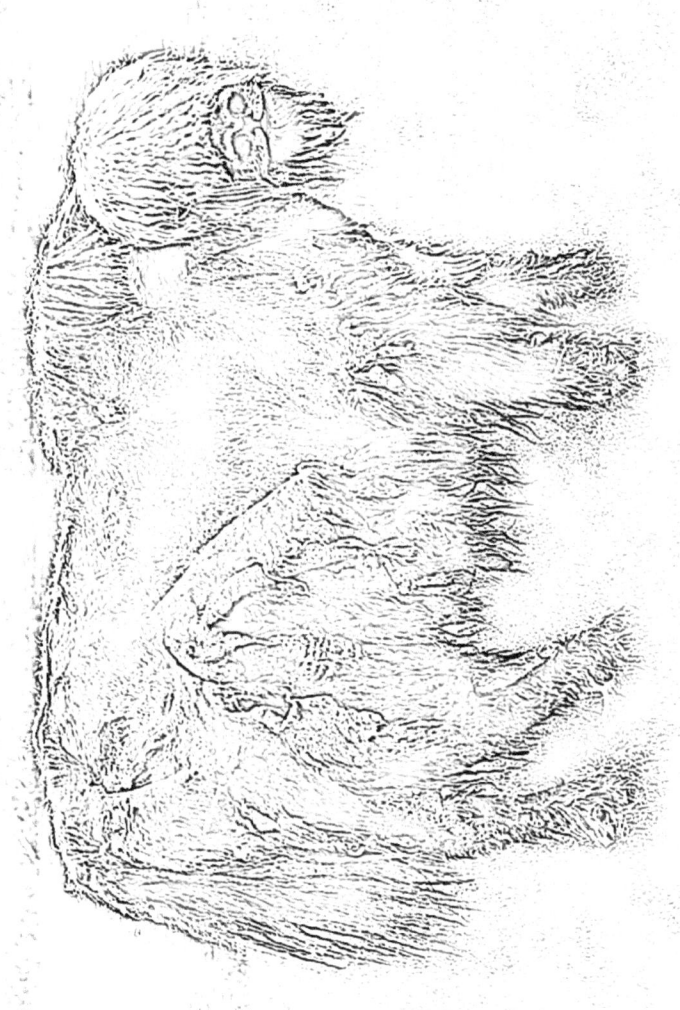

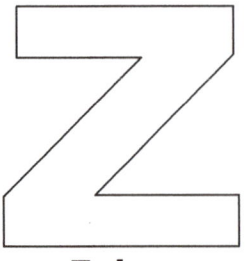

Zebra

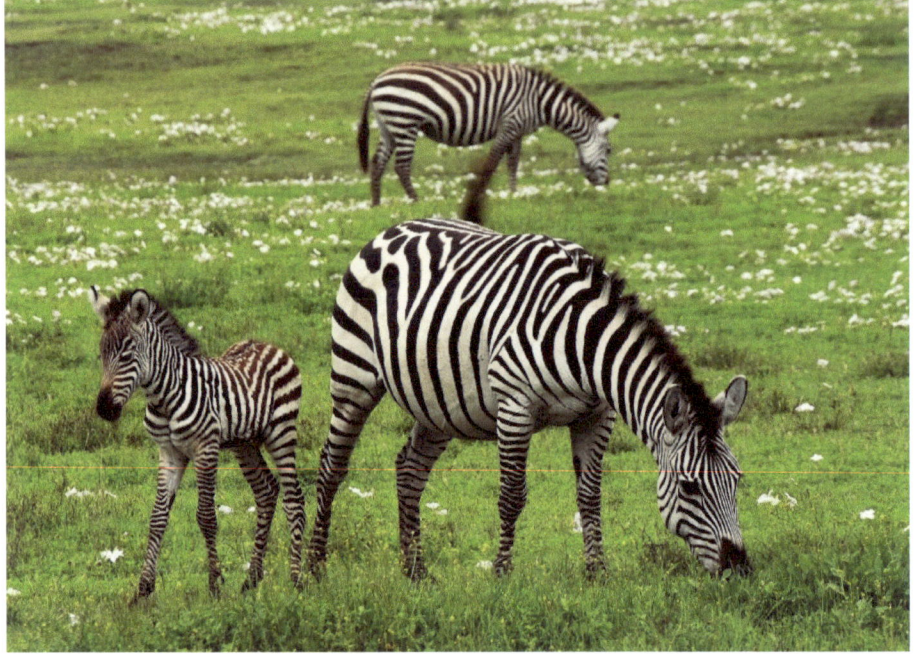

This image is of two common zebra and a foul grazing in Tanzania.

Zebras are the largest and most distinctive of wild horses. Every zebras' stripes are unique to themselves in their placement. The three different species of Zebra found in Africa are the Common Zebra, the Grevy's Zebra, and the Mountain Zebra.

*(National Geographic, Zebra,
.http://animals.nationalgeographic.com/animals/mammals/zebra/)*

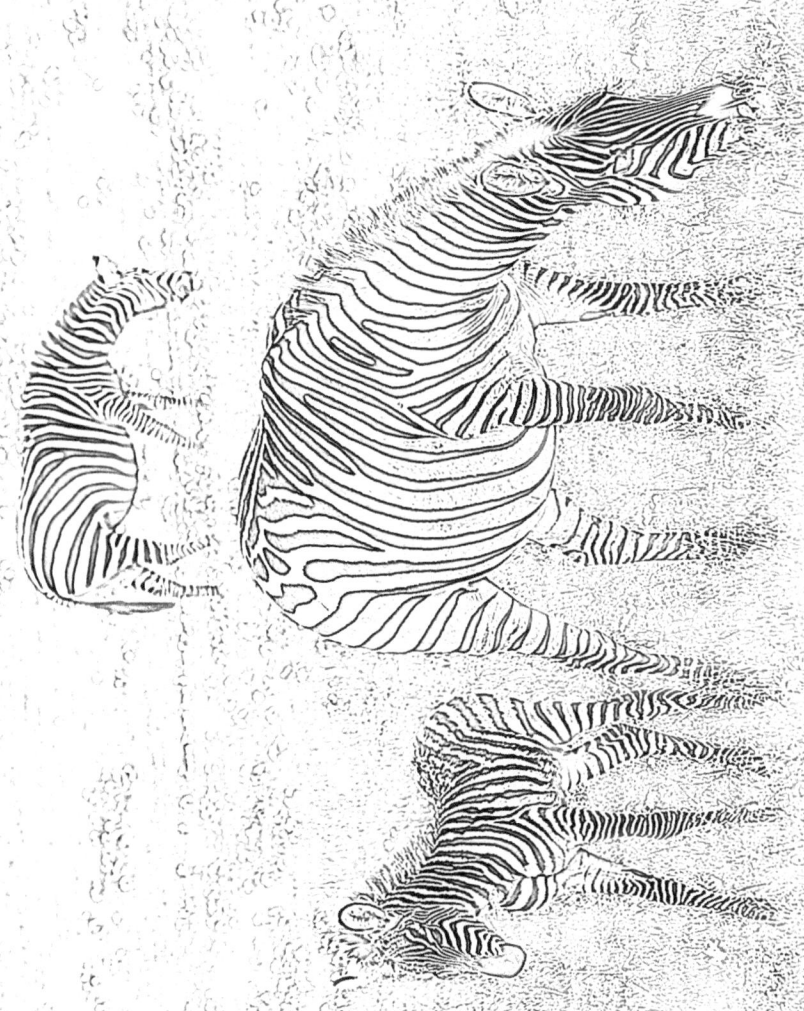